the
thorny
grace
of it

Other Books by Brian Doyle

Leaping: Revelations & Epiphanies

Mink River

Grace Notes

The Grail

The Wet Engine

Bin Laden's Bald Spot & Other Stories

Spirited Men

Epiphanies & Elegies

Credo

Reading in Bed

the thorny grace of it

And Other Essays for Imperfect Catholics

Brian Doyle

LOYOLA PRESS.
A JESUIT MINISTRY
Chicago

LOYOLA PRESS.
A JESUIT MINISTRY

3441 N. Ashland Avenue
Chicago, Illinois 60657
(800) 621-1008
www.loyolapress.com

Cover art credit: ©iStockphoto.com/Oleg Saenko, Tetra Images/Getty Images,
©iStockphoto.com/Jonathan Estrella.

Back cover author photo credit: Jerry Hart

ISBN-13: 978-0-8294-3906-9
ISBN-10: 0-8294-3906-4
Library of Congress Control Number: 2013940993

Printed in the United States of America.
13 14 15 16 17 18 Versa 10 9 8 7 6 5 4 3 2 1

For my generous kindhearted patient brother Tom,
with love and respect

contents

notes

Notes on blessed boots, defiant courage, thorny grace, sudden songs, and the brilliant burble of shy miraculous amazing children

Most of these pieces first appeared in magazines and newspapers in America, Australia, and Ireland, and I thank the open-minded and inordinately patient editors of *The Sun, Commonweal, U.S. Catholic, Newsday, The Christian Century, Reality, Eureka Street, A River & Sound Review, Manoa, Our Man in Boston, Brevity, Notre Dame Magazine, Notre Dame Business, America, The American Scholar, The Fine Delight, The Oregonian, Australian Catholics, The Catholic Sentinel, Syracuse University Magazine, CathNews Australia*, and *Saint Anthony Messenger* for their salty grace and obvious literary taste.

Particular and pointed thanks also to Tim Kroenert at *Eureka Street* magazine in Australia, who has endured a veritable slather of my pieces; to Michael McVeigh of *Australian Catholics*, who prodded me to write "How to Be Good" for a special issue of his riveting magazine; and to Garry Eastman of John Garratt Publishing in Australia, who importuned me somehow into committing the essay called "Fatherness." Persuasive lad, Garry.

Jesus &
Other Testy
Saints

did the jesus man die?

In the small chapel on Bleak Friday, Dark Friday, Haunted Friday, Despair Friday, I watch a small girl gape as the massive priest strides up the aisle and then shockingly sprawls prone on the floor, his face pressed against the golden wood.

This *never* happens; Father Jim always bows deeply and then strides briskly up and around the altar like he built it, but now he is sprawled out on the floor like a fallen heron or eagle or angel.

The chapel shivers with silence.

Is he okay, mama? Is he hurt? Is he sleeping?

We hid as it were our faces from him; he was despised, and we esteemed him not.

This girl is maybe three years old, I think; old enough to be riveted, not old enough to be cynical about the stunning theater of the moment.

He was wounded for our transgressions, he was bruised for our iniquities: with his stripes we are healed.

Whereas her brother is sound asleep on his mother's sparrow shoulder, his sweet drool marking a line like a river on the green meadow of her coat.

Of all the people on earth, of all the people who ever were and are and will be, how astounding, how incredible, that the one appointed to bear all ills, to carry all wounds, to stand for all, to be sacrificed and resurrected, to be both king of pain and prince of light, should be a thin Arab woodworker, a most devout and committed Jew. Do we gape in amazement at this totally odd detail as much as we should? Do we remember how wild it is that the One among us was not strong or wealthy, famous or charming, beautiful or honored, but a footloose vagrant on Roman roads, troublesome and strange? Of all the people in all the world, *that* guy? That's the last guy you would ever imagine, the last kid picked, the homeless guy with dirty feet.

Could that be the point, the genius, the secret?

Let us therefore come boldly unto the throne of grace, that we may obtain mercy, and find grace to help in time of need.

Amen to that, kid, I whisper to the gangly teenager reading Paul's letter aloud. Amen to *that*. The boy then opens his mouth and begins to sing in a baritone thicker than he is.

The naked altar, the empty yawning candleholders, the elderly priests sitting together in the rear of the chapel, the shy students, the graying neighbors.

To this end was I born, and for this cause came I into the world, that I should bear witness unto the truth. Everyone that is of the truth heareth my voice.

Even unto a small chapel on a sandy bluff over a broad river thousands of years later His voice washes over a small girl with pink Sesame Street mittens—the left with Bert's face and the right with Ernie's. On her hat, crumpled on the seat she never sits in once, is the sweet bright face of Elmo; all I can see is an eye, but I would recognize that joyous eye anywhere.

What I have written I have written.

The sigh and rustle of the congregation like a wave in the sea. The crackle of their knees as they sink to the floor as He hangs on the cross. His last instructions: Behold thy son! Behold thy mother! And the penultimate line that always makes me cry, in my dark corner, where the sight lines are such that I can see the whole trial and murder but no one can see me crying: *I thirst.*

Me too, man, I whisper. Me too. For the sepulchre is nigh at hand.

The small girl gapes again when Father Jim sings the adoration aloud, her mouth falling open just like a kid in the movies who sees something spectacular. And then when a student stands up and sings back to Father Jim, she yanks her dad's hand like a chain and he picks her up and her face beams over his shoulder like a sudden apple.

Sometimes it causes me to tremble, tremble, tremble, sings the choir.

Me too, you beautiful tall singing children, I whisper. Me too.

The shuffle of socks against the golden wood of the chapel floor. The boy in brilliant red sneakers kneeling to kiss the cross. The girl who holds her hair back with one hand as she kisses the cross. The boy who hugs it like a lover. The priest resting his forehead against it. The old man who touches it with his cane. The star basketball player who folds himself down and down to touch it with the huge nets of his hands. The shaking man whose touch is a series of taps. The shiver of silence as the priest lifts his hands in blessing but then walks away to the side, the one day all year when he will not walk triumphantly down the aisle like a hero parting a sea of smiles. The small girl puzzled as her mom and dad and drooling brother turn to leave.

Did he die, mama? Did the Jesus man die?

Yes, honey. He died.

But he gets born again? When does he get born again?

Tomorrow, says her mother, a freighted word I catch just as I follow them through the immense walnut doors of the chapel into the shocking light—the last thing you ever expect on Good Friday is to emerge from the haunted darkness into such a crisp redolent spring afternoon, this nails me every year, no matter how wet a winter it's been this day without fail is the most crystalline miracle imaginable, how ironic or momentous is that?—but as I turn to shuffle west I hear the father say faintly, almost under his breath,

Today.

Maybe he meant something else altogether, maybe he was starting to say something about prospective dinner plans or what crucial basketball game was on television or what cool playground they could stop at on the way home, but I don't think so. I think the father, young as he was, and he looked to be about thirty, said the truth; we are all born again today. You and me and the kid with the mittens and the thin Arab woodworker. Today.

ten blessings

The first person to bless my rosary was the priest who used to be my pastor. He retired finally and now he is a utility man, as he says, filling in where needed. You would be surprised at how many games you get to play even when you are a bench player, he says. He blessed my rosary in my office, cupping it in his huge left hand and blessing it with his right. You want to use your power hand for a good blessing, he said with a smile.

The second person to bless my rosary was my sister. She is a nun in a monastery near a huge river. She held it in both of her hands as if her hands were filled with holy water, and she bent her sweet grinning face down over my rosary, and prayed silently over it, and then draped it over my head as if she was presenting me with a prize, which she was.

The third person to bless my rosary was a small girl in sage country. She is six years old. Whatever it is that we call the creative force that made us all and can be seen most unadorned in children beams out of this kid with the force of a thousand suns. She put my rosary on top of her head and held it there with her right hand as she put her left hand on my face and said *I hope these beads will always have holy in them for when Mister Brian needs it*, which is a very good blessing, it seems to me.

The next person to bless my rosary was my archbishop, who is a most excellent guy, honest and funny, with an ego the size of a worn dime. He asked me to hold my rosary in both hands and

he held his hands over my rosary like a gentle tent and said *Lord,
we ask your blessing on this rosary, that it always be a conduit for
your endless mercy, a highway for your endless grace, a path for your
endless love,* which is also a very good blessing, I think.

The fifth person to bless my rosary was my mother, who is
ninety and bent over and has tennis balls on the legs of her
walker so she can move quicker. She leaned forward at the
kitchen table and moved the butter aside and took my rosary and
said *Let's go right to the Mother on this one, I have always found
the direct route refreshing,* and she smiled the wild alluring smile
that still rocks my dad when she aims it at him, he says it's like
someone flashing high beams at you suddenly on a dark road,
and she said *Mary, holy one, I ask your blessing on these beads and
this boy, that he always brings his light to bear against the dark,* and
then she handed the rosary back to me and flashed that song of
a smile and said now be a dear and get me the milk.

The next person to bless my rosary was a friend of mine who
is a minister on a moist island and has two tattoos where he can
see them easily all day long, *practice resurrection* on the inside of
his left forearm and *what we need is here* on the inside of his right
forearm, both lines from the Kentucky visionary Wendell Berry.
The minister and I were driving in his truck and we came to a
stoplight and I asked him to bless my rosary and he said sure and
pulled over by a laundromat and cupped my rosary against his
sweatshirt and prayed over it silently and then handed it back to
me with a smile; as he did so I read his right arm and thought of
Saint Catherine of Siena's remark, *all the way to heaven is heaven,*
which would also be an excellent line to tattoo on your forearm,
I think.

The seventh person to bless my rosary was an abbot with
whom I was sitting by a pond, the two of us engaged in what

he calls dragonfly prayer, which consists of watching dragonflies quarter the pond *very* carefully for a while, until, as he says, your appreciation of the incredible work of the creator is recharged. We do this once in a while when I am bleak and dry. One time he called me when *he* was dark and weary and asked me to come out and sit by the pond with him, which I did. When I asked him to bless my rosary he said sure and he stood and held it out over the edge of the pond and prayed silently and handed it back to me and we watched the dragonflies for a long time.

The next person to bless my rosary was an ebullient friend who is a nun and used to be a roaring drunk and says she still is although she doesn't drink anymore. She blessed my rosary in a coffee shop and like my mom she went right to the Madonna with the request. She says she and the Madonna are the best of friends from way back and they talk twice a day *and when you are desperately thirsty She is the cool clean water that saves your life, trust me*, and I do.

The ninth person to bless my rosary was a small priest who was sitting on the porch of a villa named for the Madonna. He and I were watching parrots in the enormous gum trees, and he pointed out a wallaby in the leaf litter, and when I asked him to bless my rosary he did so silently, with his eyes closed, and then he told me about blessing rosaries for the children he used to teach on the island, some of those rosaries were made from seashells, he said, and some from galip nuts, *and more than once I saw rosaries made from bullet casings*.

The tenth person to bless my rosary was the woman who played the violin at the funeral of the mother of the woman who married me. That violinist played that violin so passionately, so deftly, so delightedly, that when I went over after the funeral to thank her and express my amazement at her amazing grace I

jesus christ:
the missing
years

You know the story: we see Him at age twelve in the temple, giving his parents lip, and then we do not see Him again for eighteen years, until He goes on an extended speaking tour, seemingly finishing His run in Jerusalem, but then, stunningly, not.

But with total respect for the excellent opening of the story (an extraordinary and graceful mother, a patient and open-minded stepfather, a momentous star, a redolent manger) and for the revolutionary ending (sobbing in a dark garden, betrayal by His best friend, tortured in prison, His spirit surrendered with a loud cry of despair as the veil of the temple was rent in twain from the top to bottom and there was a darkness upon the land, resurrection!), it is those missing eighteen years that I wish to explore here, because I do not think we speculate enough about the teenaged Jesus Christ, which I feel we should, partly because I believe it will add even more awe and reverence to the awe and reverence we already feel for His poor parents, bless their memories.

First theory: Jesus was sent to His room for eighteen years, for being so incredibly sassy in the temple. His mother handles the situation with her usual calm grace, but I have always imagined His stepfather standing behind her, glowering and making stern gestures with his hands as big and strong as shovels. Remember that the man was by some accounts a fine carpenter, and my experience of fine carpenters is that they have grips of steel.

Second theory: Jesus was not sent to His room, but was placed under gentle house arrest, and spent those years home-schooling with His mom and working assiduously as an apprentice in the carpentry shop. Imagine what you could get for chairs and tables and candlesticks clearly and incontrovertibly marked as being made by Yeshuah ben Joseph of Nazareth.

Third theory: His parents did their best to ignore the sass in the temple, and Jesus did all sorts of interesting things that didn't make the papers, like play rec league basketball, and conduct tin-can drives, and try to start a falconry business with two friends, which looked promising until one friend went to Boston College and the other went into ballooning.

Fourth theory: Jesus took off with a backpack and a stave and a tattered Old Testament to see the world, walking east through the lands of the Ammonites into Arabia and Persia and thence eventually to India and Nepal and Tibet, where He spent some years in contemplation and prayer and discernment, returning to Judea eventually, perhaps, by sea. Boy: *there's* a novel.

Fifth theory: From the age of thirteen, when a boy in Jewish tradition enters manhood, to the age of thirty, when a boy in Irish-American tradition enters manhood, He was exactly the sort of young man you would expect the Son of Light to be, unbelievably thoughtful and helpful with His parents and maybe many brothers, a Godsend to his aging stepfather in the shop, a beloved and popular neighbor and friend; the kind of kid who fixes other kids' bicycles for free and has a working air pump for deflated footballs, that kind of kid. The kind of kid you want to surreptitiously detest for being such an exemplar but you can't help but love him because he actually is what he seems to be, which is rare and delightful. That kind of kid.

Sixth theory: He lay in the weeds for eighteen years, biding His time, preparing for the work He knew He was to do, the work that would leave him sobbing in a dark garden, betrayed by His best friend, tortured in prison, nailed to a cross, soldiers jeering, His mother weeping by His feet, the work that would change the world, the work that would change the course of history, the work that could even now rise like a lovely tide and sweep away despair and make violence a memory and greed a joke. Perhaps He spent those years gathering His courage about Him like a cloak for the dark day He would need it most. Perhaps He spent every minute of those eighteen years staring hungrily at the miracle of this world, its sparrows and sheep, rain and wheat, seething and snoring, His mother's eyes green as the sea, His father's grin broad as a barn. Perhaps no man—for He was a man, He was one of us, He was us, He *is* us—ever savored the shaggy wonder of the world as much as He did, for not only did He know the day He would leave it, only thirty-three years old, but He also knew the terrible price of its salvation; and must have wondered if He was man enough to pay that price, if His love was indeed as He prayed it was, deeper and wider than even the incomprehensible sea of the stars.

We sing His birth every year, a light from the darkness, life born again where all seemed dark and lost; and we mourn His death every year, a light seemingly extinguished, but reborn against all sense. But today, for once, consider the long years He alone knew His fate, and did His best to rise to it, and must have shivered, some evenings, sitting on a hill outside Nazareth, at how achingly beautiful and sweet the world is, a gift beyond price. Consider a quiet teenager on a hill—the first wisps of a mustache shy on His lip, His feet growing bigger by the minute, His heart bursting with love for the world He would have to save by leaving it. Poor boy. Brave boy.

how to be
good

First, pick up your wet towel and at least, for heavenssake, hang it up to dry. And wipe the sink after you shave. The sink doesn't have to be shining and spotless, that would be fussy and false, but at least don't leave little mounds of your neck hairs like dead insects for your partner and children to find. At least do *that*. It's the little things; they aren't little. You knew that. I am just reminding you. Like the dead sparrow that the old lady across the street picked up from the street, where it fell broken and almost unrecognizable, and she saw it as a holy being and she gently dug it into her garden of fading flowers. A little act, but it wasn't little. It sang quietly of respect and reverence for what had been alive and was thus holy beyond our ken. Or in the morning, when you rush into the shop for coffee, at least say *thank you* to the harried girl with the Geelong Cats logo tattooed on her forehead. At least look her in the eye and be gentle. Christ liveth in her, remember? Old Saint Paul said that, and who are we to gainsay the testy little gnarled genius? And the policeman who pulls you over for texting while driving, yes, you are peeved, and yes, he could be chasing down murderers, but be kind. Remove the bile from your tongue. For one thing, it actually *was* your fault, you could have checked the scores later, and for another, Christ liveth in him. Also in the grumpy imam, and

in the surly teenager, and in the raving man under the clock at
Flinders Street Station, and in the foulmouthed man at the footy,
and in the cousin you detest with a deep and abiding detestation
and have detested since you were tiny mammals fresh from the
wombs of your mothers. When he calls to ask you airily to help
him lug that awful vulgar elephantine couch to yet another of
his shabby flats, do not roar and use vulgar and vituperative language, even though you have excellent cause to do so and who
could blame you? But Christ liveth in him. Speak hard words
into your closet and cast them thus into oblivion. Help him with
the couch, for the ninth blessed time, and do not credit yourself with good works, for you too are a package of small sins
and cowardices, and the way to be good is not to join the Little
Sisters of the Poor in Calcutta, but to be half an ounce better
a man today than you were yesterday. Do not consider tomorrow. Consider the next moment after you read this essay. Do
the dishes. Call your mother. Coach the kids' team. Purge that
closet of the clothes you will never wear and give them away. Sell
the old machinery and turn it into food for those who starve.
Express gratitude. Offer a quiet prayer for broken and terrified
children. Write the minister and ask him to actually do the job
he was elected to do, which is care for the bruised among us, not
pose on television. Pray quietly by singing. We do not know how
prayers matter but we know that they matter. Do not concern
yourself with measuring and calculating, but bring your kindness and humor like sharp swords against the squirm of despair
and violence. The Church is you. Christ liveth in you. Do not
cloak Him but let Him be about His business, which is using
the tools the Creator gave you and only you to bring what light
you can. You know this. I am only reminding you. Work with all
your grace. Reach out. Do not rest. There will be time and time

enough for rest. Care for what you have been given. Give away that which you treasure most. The food of the spirit is love given and granted; savor that and disburse that which is not important. Use less, slow down, write small notes. All the way to heaven is heaven, said old Catherine of Siena, and who are we to gainsay that slight smiling genius? Remember that witness is a glorious and muscular weapon. What you see with your holy eyeballs and report with the holy twist of your tongue has weight and substance. If you see cruelty, call it by its true name. If you hear a lie, call it out in the open. Try to forgive even that which is unforgivable. That is the way forward for us. I do not know how that can be so but it is so. You and I know that. I am only reminding us. Be who only you are. Rise to what you dream. Do not cease to dream. Do not despair even though pain comes hand in hand with joy. That is the nature of the gift we were given. It is the most amazing and extraordinary and confusing and complicated gift that ever was. Never take it for granted, not for an instant, not for the seventh of a second. The price for it is your attentiveness and generosity and kindness and mercy. Also humor. Humor will destroy the brooding castles of the murderers and chase their armies wailing into the darkness. What you do now, today, in these next few minutes, matters more than I can tell you. It advances the universe two inches. If we are our best selves, there will come a world where children do not weep and war is a memory and violence is a joke no one tells, having forgotten the words. You and I know this is possible. It is what He said could happen if we loved well. He did not mean loving only the people you know. He meant every idiot and liar and thief and blowhard and even your cousin. I do not know how that could be so, but I know it is so. So do you. Let us begin again, you and me, this afternoon. Ready?

jessed blesus!

Probably my single favorite memory from teaching Sunday school, at the harried request of my pastor, who lost his usual Sunday School teacher suddenly when she married a Hindu doctor and converted on her honeymoon, was the time a small girl—this was a child named, I kid you not, Philomena—said to me, in her glorious piping voice exactly like the voice of a wren if the wren was four feet tall with a ponytail, *Jessed Blesus!* in answer to a question of mine that required the answer Blessed Jesus, for reasons I cannot now recall.

However I do recall, as clearly as I can remember anything in my long life, standing there at the front of the classroom, trying not to fall down laughing, trying to be respectful to and protective of Philomena against the blast of howling merriment from the rest of the class, and trying to keep my brain in its brainpan, although it desperately wanted to sprint off giggling and contemplate the implications for Christianity and human history if the Thin Mysterious Genius had been called Blesus rather than Jesus. Also a large percentage of my addled being wanted to then and there contemplate nomenclature (the evangelists Blatthew, Blark, Bluke, and Blohn, or Saint Belizabeth of Hungary, and things like that), but I had to pull myself together, because Philomena, who usually couldn't care less about slings and arrows from her classmates, was starting to look a little shaky. And I really liked Philomena, who had once said to me that the greatest basketball player who ever played would have been the Madonna "if she had bothered to try, but she was *busy*," so I quelled the class with my Dad Voice, the one that frightens dogs and birds if I use it outdoors, and we went back to studying holiness and grace.

After class, though, Philomena and I had a good long talk. Her mom, I had learned, lived on interstellar time, and if she said she would be at the door of the class to pick up her daughter at two, that meant 2:44, although I had come to appreciate her creative excuses, and have often thought that I could never have written novels without the experience of Philomena's mom, who once used the phrase *zoo emergency* to me, two words that still warm me on cold mornings when I think of them, usually while shaving. I have several times cut myself shaving after remembering the words *zoo emergency*. Try it for yourself, if you want. Just be careful.

Philomena knew full well that the class had laughed at her because she *transpoised* the words, as she said, but her attitude to matters of this sort was that people in general were a little too fussy about vowels and consonants marching in proper order, and if you not only got the sense of what she was trying to communicate, but also a little zest and verve of novelty, well, that wasn't so bad, was it? I agreed wholeheartedly with her about this, although as her teacher, and a man who really liked and admired her, I did make clear that goofing and riffing on language was one thing if you knew the rules and regulations, but another if you did not, the latter being a slippery slope that would lead to the fifth circle of hell, where everyone wears Los Angeles Lakers jerseys.

She agreed that she ought to know the rules and regulations, and I assigned her some admirably clear and rhythmic reading as homework (any three chapters of the New Testament, in the King James translation, for the burly shouldery prickly cadence of it, which I thought she would enjoy), and then we spent about ten minutes happily riffing on names and words that we thought might wake up a little if we edited them a bit, "temperaturar- ily," as Philomena said—things like the man in the blycamore tree, and the Book of Blisaiah—and then her mom came, at 2:44 on the button. I do not know what planet it is that operates exactly forty-four minutes later than this one, but it must be a very interesting planet indeed.

every other thursday evening except during holy week . . .

. . . The Saint Francis de Sales Parish Book Club meets in the basement room in the rectory where Father Matthias used to run the parish weightlifting club, until he was recruited by the local Lutheran university football team to be their strength and conditioning coach, which he says cheerfully is a ministry among the heathen not unlike Saint Thomas sweating amid the Hindus on the teeming shores of India, although the Lutherans, God bless their tall souls, are a sect founded by a Catholic monk, so we must remember they are our cousins in the Merciful Lord Jesus, and besides, old Martin Luther did say *sin boldly*, for which you have to admire the old reprobate.

*Any*way, says Mrs. Cooney, notwithstanding Father Matt's convoluted apologetics here, we are *not* here to talk about Father Matt, who remains a priest in good standing even if he is bulking up Lutherans, despite what certain unnamed members of the Altar Society twitter in scurrilous fashion, but we *are* here to decide what books to read this fall, before we return to the collected works of the greatest Catholic novelist of all time, who is of course Maeve Binchy. The floor is open.

The plays of His Holiness the late John Paul II!

Great pope, awful playwright, says Mrs. Cooney. No. Next.

The essays of Andre Dubus?

Yes. Best Catholic writer since Flannery O'Connor.

Should we read his stories also?

No. Adultery every third page. He's the American Graham Greene.

James Joyce?

Well—he wasn't Catholic after puberty. Maybe *Dubliners*.

Merton's *The Seven Storey Mountain*!

No. Overwritten boyish burble. A good editor would have halved it.

Objection! It totally caught the Catholic zeitgeist of the 1950s!

Anyone using the word *zeitgeist* loses her vote, says Mrs. Cooney coldly. Next.

Ron Hansen's novel *Mariette in Ecstasy*?

Is that . . . lurid? If so I vote yes.

No, no—life in a convent, awe, jealousy, stigmata. Glorious stuff.

Approved, says Mrs. Cooney. Which reminds me that we should also have Rumer Godden's *In This House of Brede* on the list. Masterpiece. Set in an abbey.

Dorothy Day's diaries?

Yes. *What* a witness to the miracle of every moment.

Flannery O'Connor's letters?

Yes. Maybe the only writer other than Robert Louis Stevenson whose letters are not about money. Writers—what a bunch of whiners.

Chesterton?

No. Poor man never had an unpublished thought. Let's not reward him for that.

Waugh?

No, he's English. No imperial slavemasters this year.

Annie Dillard?

Yes. Maybe *Pilgrim at Tinker Creek*, right after Dorothy Day, as a sort of witness to wonder theme. Then maybe *For the Time Being*, which is weird and glorious.

Teilhard de Chardin?

No. Incomprehensible. Not even Teilhard knew what he was talking about, the poor man. Plus he was a Jesuit, and we are focusing on Catholic writers this year.

George Bernanos?

No. No one admits how dull *Diary of a Country Priest* is.

Carlo Levi?

No. Humorless.

Primo Levi?

Yes. Another one for our witness to grace theme. Can you witness evil and report on it in such a way that no one can ever forget what happened ever again, which is a blow against the darkness? Yes.

Joseph Bernardin?

Yes. That man was a saint.

J. F. Powers?

Yes. Let's read all of Powers. Half-forgotten, and undeservedly so. As fine a Catholic fiction writer as this country ever hatched from its salty soil, period.

Fulton Sheen?

No. You know the rules: no writers who wore heavy makeup.

Paul Wilkes' *In Mysterious Ways: The Death and Life of a Parish Priest?*

Yes.

Mary Gordon?

Yes.

Walker Percy?

Yes.

Myles Connolly's *Mr. Blue?*

No. No campus novels. Even Nabokov couldn't do it well.

Willa Cather's *Death Comes for the Archbishop?*

Yes. Perfection. Leanest great novel ever.

LeBron James?

Not Catholic, hasn't written a masterpiece yet. Mrs. Warren, how many books are on the list now?

Seven thousand.

No, really.

Thirty.

That should take us through the first month. Let's keep going.

Alice McDermott!

Ooooooooo, great choice. The great Catholic novelist of our time. We'll start with *Charming Billy* and then go to *At Weddings and Wakes* and finish with *After This*. Triptych.

Gesundheit.

The King James Bible?

Isn't that missing a couple of key chapters?

Yes, but my heavens, the muscular edgy prose—makes all the other translations sound like singing into a bowl of oatmeal.

Well—maybe the second half, the good part, says Mrs. Cooney. So there's the winter taken care of. Spring books?

Do they have to be by Catholic writers?

No—we already have Primo Levi, and he was Italian. But let's stay with witness to grace.

Wendell Berry's essays?

Yes.

David James Duncan's *God Laughs & Plays*!

Terrific choice. Although didn't he grow up Seventh-Day Adventist?

Yes, but he recovered.

You know why the Seventh-Day Adventists frown on pre-marital sex?

Why?

Might lead to dancing.

Alright, alright. Other suggestions?

The Shawl by Cynthia Ozick.

Great choice. But we can read that haunting story in ten minutes. Although maybe we should focus on shorter works in the spring. Sap rising and all that. Young men's fancies turning to love and hockey.

Mark Twain's essay "The War Prayer."

Yes.

Merton's poem "Original Child Bomb."

Yes.

LeBron James!

No.

Chet Raymo.

Good choice. I nominate *Climbing Brandon*. A thin masterpiece. Like David Bowie.

Mary Oliver?

Is she Catholic?

No, but she's the great American poet of our time, and attentiveness is the beginning of all prayer, as she says, and

Catholicism really is about attentiveness as the crucial step in witnessing and celebrating the extraordinary generosity of God to us, His mewling and muddled children. Therefore Mary Oliver, one might conclude, is the great Catholic poet of our time, other than Bruce Springsteen.

Is that kind of reasoning legal?

Isn't that hermeneutical?

Herman who?

Can you be Catholic if you are from New Jersey?

Can Father Matt make a Lutheran so big that not even Father Matt can lift him?

If a Muslim man becomes a mathematician and a musician, is he Islamamathemusical?

I think we have come to the end of the useful part of this meeting, says Mrs. Cooney, with the faintest hint of a smile. Mrs. Warren, what's our total?

Fifty thousand.

No, really.

Forty.

Motion to adjourn? We just have time to open our Witness to Grace season upstairs in the den—LeBron James is on, and Father Matt says he'll give a short talk about the Los Angeles Lakers as the evil spawn of the Dark One. First assignment, then, to be read by next Thursday: Andre Dubus's *Meditations from a Movable Chair*.

Wasn't he a Red Sox fan? Isn't that Calvinist?

Enough, says Mrs. Cooney firmly. Game time. Do we have enough beer glasses?

Is that a rhetorical question?

Herman who?

confessio

I, Brian, a sinner, a most simple suburbian, a generally decent sort but subject to fits of unrelieved selfishness, do here wish to confess and be shriven, in such a manner that speaking of that which I have not done well will provoke me to do better; this slight daily improvement being exactly the work we are asked to do by the Shining One. So then:

I missed my cousin's funeral because I had girlfriend plans that I was not man enough to break; and this beloved cousin was a nun, and to this day, nearly thirty years after I casually blew off her funeral, I am haunted by the story of my sister, also now a nun, leaving a small bowl of white flowers on the altar after the Mass, because she and our cousin loved small white flowers, which they felt were overlooked in the world, but which often arrived first and smelled best.

Obsecro ut mihi ignoscas, I beg to be forgiven.

Also I was for many years sneering and dismissive and vulgar and rude to my mother and father, never once seeing the pain I inflicted, never once thinking of them as human beings, never once thinking how they would feel to have raised and coddled a child with such a serpent's tongue; and not until I was nineteen did I feel the lash of remorse, and pick up the telephone, and apologize profusely, and ask their forgiveness for years of surly lip.

Obsecro ut mihi ignoscas.

Also I did for years actually take my lovely bride for granted, more than a little; I did think that being married meant that she would never leave me and I could drift into a gentle self-ishness that she would have to endure because she had sworn in public in a church before many witnesses *to be true in good times and bad, in sickness and health, to love and honor you all the days of my life*, I carry those words in my wallet; but I did not look at them enough and contemplate them and mull over them and take them deep into my hoary heart and consider what they asked *me* to do and be, and there came dark years, and I was in no small part responsible for their bleakness and pain.

Obsecro ut mihi ignoscas.

Also I have roared at my children, and snarled at them, and insulted them, and made cutting remarks, and teased and razzed them past the point of gentle humor; and I have belittled their ideas and accomplishments, and failed to listen to what they were saying beneath the words they were using, and failed to contemplate their dreams, especially when their dreams were far from the dreams I had for them; and I set lofty expectations and standards and behavioral bars, all this having more to do with what I wanted than with what they wanted and who they wished to be; and a thousand thousand times I have spoken to them sternly of what they have not done rather than sweetly of what they have done, and left unsaid that which I feel most certainly in my heart, this being a love so oceanic and electric that I cannot find words for it, though I would happily die for them anytime anyhow anywhere, and if that is so, as I know it to be so, why can I not be more gentle to them, instead of barking about the failed test?

Obsecro ut mihi ignoscas.

Also I have gossiped and committed calumny and made snide remarks about friends and acquaintances, and made snap judgments based on appearance, and held people to higher standards than I could meet myself, and jumped to conclusions based on no evidence at all not even ephemeral and circumstantial; and offered scurrilous insults freely; and while hiding behind humor actually flicked words like whips and chains upon those who deserved nothing of the sort; and I have amused myself with dark remarks; and I have often amused myself at the expense of others, under the guise of laughter; and I have done this so very much, I realize, because it is so very uncomfortable to say this aloud here on the naked page.

Obsecro ut mihi ignoscas.

Also I have taken seats on the bus reserved for the elderly and weary when I was neither; and I have sat mute on the bus while old women stood awkwardly, their heavy bags battering their thin shoulders; and I have stolen shampoo and notepads and pens from hotels and motels; and I have even stolen a Gideon Bible from a motel; and I have stolen vast ranks of teas from conferences and seminars; and I have stolen towels from pools and gyms; and I have stolen much else under the aegis of borrowing, knowing full well that I would never return nor attempt to return the contraband; and I have even in this way stolen obscure paperback books from the shelves of friends; another confession that makes me so uncomfortable that it must be true.

Obsecro ut mihi ignoscas.

There are many more things under heaven that I could here confess, but I am going to use the lovely excuse that time grows short and the end of the page draws near, so I beseech the reader to ascribe many more sins large and small to me, and leave them nameless except to Him who knows every feather of every

the silver
jesuses

And while we are talking about fourth grade, I am reminded of Maureen McInery's neck in front of me in the third row, that smug smarmy neck gloating and preening at me for nine long months, as day after day, week after week, she bested me in math tests and social studies projects and science experiments, finishing first in whatever academic contest had been posed to the class by Mrs. O'Malley, who looked like a linebacker with spectacles. And she, Maureen McInery, owner of that smirking neck, again and again got *her* paper back with a gold Jesus on it, whereas I earned a series of silver Jesuses as long as your arm. No boy ever accumulated such a parade of silver Jesuses as the undersigned, who brought them home day after day, week after week, Jesus glinting like a gleaming new coin from my satchel, and showed them to my mom, who tried her best to pretend that a silver Jesus was every bit as good as a gold Jesus. *At least it is not a bronze Jesus*, she actually said once, a line I remember because I never heard that sentence before (or since), and because my brother Thomas had earned a bronze Jesus in kindergarten *that very morning*, apparently for not peeing on himself, for once, or perhaps for managing to eat his lunch without incurring injury, for a change. You wouldn't believe how many times this kid started out to eat a candy bar and ended up with a cast on his arm, or tried to open the peanut butter jar and finished by using the last seven bandaids in the pantry to stanch the blood, which caused my father to once again use lewd and vulgar language, which he had sworn, in front of a priest at the Nocturnal Adoration Society meeting, not to do, but did.

The bronze Jesuses in *our* class, I note, were scattered like cherry petals, cheap goods, willy nilly (and there actually *was* a kid in our class named Willie Nilley), everyone earning one eventually except Michael O'Sullivan, whose grandfather had married a Lutheran—a mixed marriage, yes, but *not* a good example of miscegenation, Michael, as Mrs. O'Malley said, tersely, while handing Maureen McInery yet another gold Jesus.

I kept my silver Jesuses for some years, in a drawer filled with Jesuses of various shapes and hues and materials: there was the Jesus patch presented to us by a visiting Jesuit one time, as a sort of team logo, and there was a small statue that may or may not have been Jesus, presented to me in sixth-grade basketball, although the coach, one of the dads, and not one of the dads who had ever played or seen basketball played before, it turned out, told me that if it *was* Jesus, which he was not totally sure it was, it was a rare case of a long lean Jesus portrayed in tight gym shorts, sculpted as if he, basketball Jesus, had just launched a jump shot, his right hand following through correctly so as to impart backspin on the ball, and his left hand serving as a guide, something like the tower that guides a rocket until the moment of liftoff, at which point the tower, or left hand, having executed its function, flies free—are you listening to what I am saying, Brian?

Anyway, the reason I tell you this story is to relate the time I set out to actually, no kidding, *steal a gold Jesus* from Maureen McInery's desk at recess. I had been driven mad by the infinite parade of silver Jesuses, and I could take no more silver Jesuses, and I set out, greed and rage in my heart, to procure a gold Jesus, come hell or high water. I say this ruefully, aware of the stench of sin, but a man must face his demons, even those that taunted him when he was ten years old, and I crept toward her desk, wondering what that awful stench was, and hoisted the lid of her desk, and found her most recent gold Jesus face-down in what appeared to be the soggy remnant of a liverwurst sandwich. Thus ended my roaring ambition for a gold Jesus unearned by personal toil and discipline, and I have been a better man since.

I think we can all agree that this is a lesson that should not be lost. When next you find yourself weary beyond words of silver Jesuses, and your dignity and discipline have dissolved to such a degree that you find yourself on your knees at recess slinking up an aisle of cracked and ancient linoleum toward a desk glowing with gold Jesuses, take it from me, your friend Brian, that this is a poor idea, not a project that will end well, and return to your seat forthwith, and face forward, with your hands where I can see them, and forget the smug prim neck of Maureen McInery; for while *you* will go on to a glittering career as a penniless essayist, *she* will eventually become a Protestant bishop or prophet, I believe somewhere in the Midwest, says my mother on the telephone. Let us say a prayer for her eternal soul. Do you still have your silver Jesuses? Did I tell you what happened to your brother Thomas yesterday?

nobody
cannot be
saints

Some weeks ago I received a letter from a girl, age eleven, in
Korea. She lives by the sea. At her school there is a shelf with
books published in the languages of English, she wrote me, and
one day she lifted one of those books up and away from its shelf
companions, perhaps struck by the bright golden spine, and she
read it in two days, and then sat down to compose an electric
letter to the author, whose electric address, as she noted, was in
the back of the book, good thing for that!

Dear Mister, she wrote, your book gave me such wise lessons. I
learned new things about saints and, also, how to love. I learned
to bend our hours into acts of love, to love not only sweet friends
and family but enemies. Well, honestly, I used to love only my
dearest people, such as friends and family. But, how about my
enemies? I used to be hostile to them. I just acted mean to them,
not even thinking about how they would feel. But now I truly
recognize that saints are here and saints are us. We, the people,
used to be stupid, looking for saints there when they are living
right here. But saints are us. Nobody cannot be saints. I now
realize that. Thank you for writing fabulous. Your book is the
best one I have read so far.

Of course I wrote back. What sort of man would not write back? I wrote back at length. I wrote about joy and amazement. I wrote about grace under duress. I wondered what the other books on that shelf by the sea in Korea might be. I wondered what her city smelled like early in the morning in those last few moments before the sun rose over the lip of the sea. I wondered what fish were in that sea. I wrote about the way it seemed to me that the most saintly and amazingly rivetingly holy people I ever met were all liable to laughter and had egos so tiny you couldn't find them with the most powerful microscopes. I wondered what other books she was reading. I wondered how my book had found its way from the snowy farmlands where it was published to a shelf of books in the languages of English in a city in Korea.

She wrote back right quick: thank you very much for giving me your response! I was full of excitement to open your electric-mail! I love your phrases! I will keep them in my mind! I want to read your books more. Are there more books that you wrote? I feel warm from your letter.

Of course I wrote back. What sort of man would not write back? I wrote back at length. I wrote about the subtle pleasure of firing a torrent of words and stories into the air and having them land in a heart by the sea on the other side of the world. I wrote about how stories matter way more than we understand, and stories are prayers of terrific power, and stories are food, and how we are actually walking stories, we are collections of stories, we are vast houses in which stories come and go, and if we don't listen for them, and savor them, and carry them in our pockets, and share them, then we have nothing, for stories are how we live, and stories are compasses and lodestars, for example the mysterious stories of the thin Jewish man who walked around telling stories a very long time ago but how amazing that His stories still persist, still unsettle, still ripple and riffle and ruffle hearts, a most astonishing and portentous state of affairs.

Thank you very much, sir, came her immediate reply. We would like to read all of your books. We would like to read all the other best books about how there are saints all around us. How do you know this? One of us wants to know.

I have met saints, I replied. I have seen miracles. I think everyone has saint seeds inside them. I think everyone knows this deep in their bones but sometimes we are frightened of what this means. I think we are as easily distracted as children from what we know to be true and right. I think we are as selfish as toddlers much of the time. I am the worst of offenders in this regard. Yet I attend to miracles and saints. I have seen saintly sides in the most unsaintly people you could imagine. Maybe no one is a saint all the time but everyone is a saint some of the time. Maybe saintliness is difficult and troublesome. Maybe that's the point of saintliness, to cause a ruckus. Maybe the word *saint* is just a label and we should be wary of trying to define or limit or explain something glorious and generous beyond articulation, like the Coherent Mercy who made you and me and the sea. I will send you all my books and hope that some of the stories inside them land in your heart and cause you joy.

Thank you so much, sir, came her reply, right quick. We hardly know how we can express our thankness to you.

Nor do I know how I can express my thankness to you, I replied. You have honored me more than you know. You have caused me great joy. We have shared some electric zest that I cannot explain but I am sure it matters very much. Perhaps our connection is yet another name for God. There are many names for God and His names slide off His joy like swallows pouring from cliffs by the sea. In the years to come I will think of you and you will think of me and that will be a good thing in ways we will never know. Isn't that wonderful? Isn't that a most excellent story?

first draft of
the first letter
to the
corinthians

Love is patient. Love is kind. Love is not jealous. Love does not steam open letters that have return addresses you think look like they were written by women when you *know* they are from my cousin, and yes, she and I kissed that one time, but we were thirteen years *old*, for heaven's sake, and I think Abraham *Lincoln* was president, that's how long ago that was. Love does not brag. Love is not arrogant. Love does not act unbecomingly, like that time you made eyes at the cello player from Cuba at that fundraising concert because you were convinced beyond the shadow of a doubt he was staring at you while he played love songs even though we were in the nosebleed section for heaven's sake, not to mention that your fan letters came back marked return to sender, not that I crowed about that overmuch. Love does not seek its own. Love is not provoked, no matter how many times I play Cuban cello music and start to laugh and you stomp off and lock yourself fuming in the bathroom. Love does not take into account a wrong suffered, even being late on the property tax payment and having to pay that penalty which

is money we would have spent in some foolish fashion anyway, trust me, perhaps on the collected works of every blessed
Cuban cello player who ever graced this blessed earth. Love
does not rejoice in unrighteousness, even when someone who
does not ordinarily overeat attempts to consume a turducken
in homage to John Madden that I admit was a terrible, terrible idea. Love rejoices with the truth, which is that I love you
in some deep strange mysterious way that has nothing much to
do with swooning and making out in the car and everything
to do with laughing together and brushing hands against your
hair when you are almost asleep just because you look like an
exhausted angel and I know you have to get up at dawn to walk
the blessed dog. Love bears all things, even turducken misadven-
tures and kitchen cabinets repaired with duct tape and Puccini
sung badly in the shower and the shower head repaired with duct
tape and not enough money and an army of teenagers—whose
idea was it to have all these children anyway it's not like we can
afford them but still what would we have been without them
other than much better rested? Love believes all things, even the
astounding idea that we are still married, love hopes all things,
like maybe the duct-tape market will collapse and someone we
will not name will actually no kidding get a screwdriver and fix
the blessed hinges on the cabinet not to mention the shower
head. Love endures all things, even stupid jokes made ten thousand times with the childish idiotic simplicity of the first time
when it wasn't funny that time either. Love never fails, even in
those moments when we are glaring at each other in the kitchen,
which there have been a few of those moments, and there will
be a few more, because love isn't a placid sea, love is a verb,
love is human, which means flawed and difficult and complex
and startling and wonderful and painful. Faith abides, for what

the scentsory
adventure

You know what no one talks about when they talk about the Mass? The panoply of scents, the plethora of sensory adventures that enter through the doors of your nose, the layered and complex and lovely subtle messages you *smell* in Mass.

For instance: the sweet intricate tendrils of incense, and the cheerfully dank aura of raincoats and moist jackets and dripping umbrellas by the door; and the faint talcumpowdery smell of the three babies in attendance; and the sharp abrupt smell of matches and lighters as candles are lit; and the ancient dignified redolence of the wooden walls and organ and pews; and the faintest hint of mothballs and incense and cigar smoke as Father sails up the aisle like a battleship draped in layers of linen and cotton; and the deep tang of the wine and sturdy floury tastelessness of the wafer; and the leathery friendly aftershaveish smell of your neighbor as he shakes your hand; and the sweet blast of perfume from your other neighbor as she shakes your hand; and the shaggy musky popcornish teenager scents as you hug your lanky sons, not yet fully awake even yet; and the coolest scent of all, the honey cinnamon coffee beach scent of your lovely mysterious bride, as you kiss her, yes, kiss her, right in the middle of Mass, before all these people, because you wish her well, and you wish her peace, and she somehow got the boys out of bed and into the car, you do not know how, for she is short and they are long, but here you all are in the pew, smelling the hundred miraculous smells that have so much to do with the deep pleasure and savor of the Mass.

Such as: the happy oily reek of doughnuts stacked in the lobby, awaiting attack from children who come in waves the second Father sails past them on his way down the aisle, so that he appears to be followed by a troop of children, bouncing behind him like brightly colored balls; and the blunt workman-like scent of coffee in urns that appear to have been purchased from the Defense Department after the First World War; and the bookish dusty serious smell of the tiny library of missals and Spiritual Literature and songbooks and even, God bless me, the collected works of Anton Chekhov for some reason; and the scent of the vast moist copse of cedar trees across the street, a scent that blows through the lobby like a tide whenever someone opens the door of the church; and the incomprehensible trust-worthy graceful scent of Father as he shakes hands and hugs children by the door; *he smells like grandfathers and apples*, as one of my small Sunday School students once said, and indeed he does.

The Mass is a work of quotidian genius in so many gentle human ways; for all we laud and bow at the miracle in it, perhaps the deeper miracle even than the Quiet Guest who arrives mid-way is the sweet shuffling gathering itself—the miracle *of* it. We collect, we rise and subside, we sing and chant, we tell stories at the table around the meal, we shake hands and kiss and hug and laugh. The scents and sounds and touches braid and weave and stitch something quietly astounding, every day, in a thou-sand languages, all over the world. This morning, with the scents of rain and cedar and babies and cigars and cinnamon and sweat and coffee and apples and trust in my nose, I say thanks.

Speaking
Catholic

the clan of
catholic

A while ago I shuffled and shambled into the noon Mass at the
university where I work, a Mass that is the most lovely lonely
thing most of the time, because usually there are a dozen people
there at most, counting the celebrant and the Special Guest who
arrives in the middle of the Mass, so there is a real meal feel to
it, the sharing of food around a table with people you know but
don't know all that well, like second cousins or neighbors from
two streets over. Plus in summer and fall there are great buttery
bars of light falling into the chapel from the high windows, and
sometimes there are swallows zooming through Mass because
the young priest who runs the chapel likes to leave the doors
propped open, and sometimes there's an addled guy who talks to
himself the whole Mass and apparently had a really colorful life
at least from what he mutters, and also I never know which of
the university's priests or visiting priests will be celebrating the
Mass, so every time you go it's a surprise to see who's driving the
bus, which is sort of cool, and one of the reasons I go.

There are a lot of other reasons I go, some of them having to
do with light and forgiveness and pain and my mom and swallows and my children and peace and the Madonna and addled
guys, of which let's face it I am one, so I go to Mass at the chapel
a lot.

The other day I wander into the chapel at exactly the instant Mass begins, and I sigh to see the celebrant, for it's the university's touchiest testiest most querulous most irascible priest, a guy whose sermons go charging off in ten directions at once, a guy who isn't at all shy about excoriating the congregation, a guy as liable to lecture for half an hour on proper attire or how exactly saints were roasted in the good old days when there *were* such creatures as saints not like *today* when all he sees are herds of contented *cows* in the chapel and no brave *crusaders* against evil and cant that *he* notices.

But you can't in good conscience tiptoe out of Mass the instant it begins, though you can, technically, tiptoe out of Mass the instant that the bread and wine have been changed into Christ—you have to witness the miracle, that's a given—but leaving because you don't like the celebrant, that's bad form, so I sit down, and Mass begins, and very soon, for the thousandth time in my rumpled life, I am entranced by the simple human genius and theater of the Mass, the way it is a series of stories, a fabric of voices, a braiding of experience and witness, a commitment to the illogical and nonsensical. We have a sliver of bread and a sip of wine and we shake hands. A woman who doesn't sing very well sings two songs and a man who doesn't read very well aloud reads aloud. The shabby singing and ragged reading move me more than I can explain. As I get older it's the small things that seem the biggest to me, and the fact that the singer can't find the key and the reader mumbles seem unutterably sweet.

During the Mass I notice the testy priest fumbling a bit for his cruets and the right page of the text, and he seems distracted when he gives his (blessedly short and sensible) sermon, and I notice that when he shakes hands he lets people come to him rather than go to them or sprint around the chapel pumping hands as I saw a young priest do once, but I don't think much about it, he's older than dirt and probably feeling Paleozoic this morning. But then I watch for a moment after the ceremony, as he undoes his vestments and puts away book, chalice, clothes; I watch him carefully reaching for things and feeling his way around the room; and I realize he's blind.

I've known this man for years. He's charming, a grouch, brilliant, fascinating, frustrating, petty, generous; and he is also, I now realize, a consummate actor. He's been slowly going blind for years, and because he is prickly proud and wishes to still be of service, he told no one, and now he's as blind as a door, and I'll tell no one.

He shuffles quickly out of the chapel and off to lunch, which he never misses—he never misses any meal whatsoever, but you can't imagine where the food goes, he's skinny as a stick—and I watch him shuffle off down a sidewalk he has used for fifty years, and I turn and go right back into the chapel to ask forgiveness for being such a boneheaded wooden-hearted impatient arrogant mulish stump of a man. I talk to the Madonna for a while and as usual I do all the talking and Herself does all the listening and then I just sit and watch the buttery bars of light.

I think about the motley chaotic confusing house that is Catholicism. I think about the mad wondrous prayer of the Mass. I think about how there are such stunning and wonderful and confusing people in the clan of Catholic. I think about how we are all several kinds of people at once and hardly know ourselves let alone anybody else. I think about how *possible* the Church is, and how possible we are. I think about how really the Church is just lots and lots of us mulish miracles gathered for little holy meals and story-swaps. I think about how religions are like people, capable of both extraordinary evil and unimaginable grace. I think about how the Church is sort of like the windows above me which catch these timbers of sun and focus them on the human comedy. I think about how I'd be a lot less of a man if I didn't have ways to wake up to what I can be if I harness mercy and humor and wisdom and attention and prayer and humility and courage and grace.

Which is what all true stories are about. Which is what we are, really, at our best—true stories. And true stories, stories with love and power in them, can save your life and save your soul and bring you, if even for only a flickering instant, face-to-face with the unimaginable creative force that once, a very long time ago, explained itself to Moses as, simply and confusingly, *I Am Who Am*. That force is in you, in every moment, in every story; which you know and I know, and which we hardly ever admit, which we should, so I do, amen.

a rosary

I'll tell you a story about one rosary and let it stand for so very many of these lovely silent haunting companions in our pockets and cars and purses and drawers and under pillows and wrapped in the hands of the dead.

This rosary was made eighty years ago by a boy in the woods of Oregon. He was a timber cutter working so deep in the woods that there were no roads and the men and boys rode into camp on mules. He was seventeen years old that summer and very lonely and one evening he began to carve rosary beads from cedar splits otherwise destined for the fire. He tried to carve a bead a night, sitting by the fire, and with each bead he would try to remember the story of the bead as his mother had told him. There were the joyful mysteries of good news and visiting cousins and new babies and christenings and finding children whom you feared were lost utterly. There were the sorrowful mysteries of men weeping in the dark and men beating men and men jeering and taunting men and men torturing men and men murdering men under the aegis of the law. There were the glorious mysteries of life defeating death and light returning against epic darkness and epiphanies arriving when no doors or windows seemed open to admit them and love defeating death and the victory of that we know to be true against all evidence that it is not.

When he had cut a bead for each of these stories he was finished, for there were at that time no luminous mysteries on which to ponder and pray.

He threaded thin copper wire through each of the beads, setting the mysteries apart with larger beads cut from yew, and he carved a cross from the shinbone of an elk, and he thought about trying to carve a Christ also, but the thought of carving Christ made him uncomfortable, and anyway he did not think he had the skill, and he did not want to ask one of the older men, some of whom were superb carvers, so he left the cross unadorned, as he said, and put the rosary in his pocket, and carried it with him every day the rest of his life.

The rosary went with him through Italy and North Africa in the war, and into the wheat fields of Oregon, and back into the woods where he again cut timber for a while, and then all through his travels as a journalist on every blessed muddy road from Canada to California, as he said, and through his brief but very happy years in retirement by the sea, where his rosary acquired a patina of salt from the mother of all oceans, as he said.

He had the rosary in his pocket the day he was on his knees in his garden and leaned forward and placed his face upon the earth and died, almost seventy years after he finished carving the rosary in the deep woods as a boy.

His wife carried the rosary in her pocket for the next two years until the morning she died in her bed, smiling at the prospect of seeing her husband by evening, as she told their son.

The son carried the rosary in his pocket for the next three days until the moment when he and I were walking out of the church laughing at one of his father's thousand salty stories of life in the woods and in the war and in the fields and on the road and by the sea, at which point the son handed it to me, said *Dad wanted you to have it,* and hustled away to attend to his wife and children, brothers and nieces and nephews.

I wept. Sure I did. You would weep too. Sure, you would.

I have the rosary in my pocket now. I hope to carry it every day the rest of my life, and jingle it absentmindedly, and pray it here and there when I have a moment in the sun, and place it ever so carefully and gently on a shelf every night before I go to bed, touching the elk-bone cross with a smile in memory of my friend George, until the morning of my own death, when I pray for a last few moments of grace in which to hand it to my son, and then close my eyes and go to see the One for whom it was made, who made us, amen.

the true story
of *catholic golf digest*

My friend Pete, who is such an entrepreneur that he actually no kidding sold Band-Aids at inflated prices to kids he tripped deliberately in the playground when he was in kindergarten, had a brainstorm recently and invented *Catholic Golf Digest* magazine, which led, in rapid succession, to *The Catholic Plumber, The Catholic Florist,* jazzwithjesus.com, and the short-lived but enormously famous Jesus Is Back Pop-Up Books For Children!, which is a great Easter gift but there were some unfortunate design and manufacturing problems such that when a kid opened the book Jesus shot across the room like a bearded arrow, and there was that unfortunate incident when a kid in Michigan opened a book and Jesus leaped out and got so mangled by the ceiling fan that the kid became a Hindu and the lawsuit is still in arbitration. But this note is about *Catholic Golf Digest,* which has become such a cultural phenomenon that the need arises for some factual machete-work through the thicket of rumor surrounding the magazine.

It is not true, for example, that the only recent pope with a decent iron game was the late great John Paul II, nor is it true that JPII grimly lashed three-irons at the office windows of the

Polish Communist government before he celebrated his famous 1979 Mass in Warsaw, the one where he shouted *I cry from all the depths of this millennium, let your Spirit descend!* which still gives me the happy shivers; it was a wedge, chosen because he had to play off cobblestones. Nor is it true that His Holiness Pope Emeritus Benedict XVI carried a brassie with him to discipline wayward theologians. It *is* true that Bernard Cardinal Law, formerly of the Archdiocese of Boston, was the worst golfer in the history of the universe, and birds and caddies quailed when His Eminence hoisted his bag for a pastoral afternoon on the links, for the man couldn't hit the broad side of an ocean liner if it was docked four feet away, plus he fudged his score, and claimed he carried no cash when he lost a bet, slapping his purple robes melodramatically for effect. We have all met such men, and there is a special place in New Jersey for them.

As regards the controversy about Jesus and his short game, no, the magazine did *not* claim that He was a lefty and had a feathery touch around the greens, for the simple reason that there *were no golf courses in Judea at the time*, and no one but His entourage knows if He indeed, as rumored, spent an hour every morning before office hours hitting flop shots with a huge cigar clenched in the divine grillwork, although that rumor did eventually lead my friend Pete to start *The Catholic Dentist*, which has done well and spawned a whole subseries of e-newsletters for devout orthodontists and anesthesiologists and suchlike. I confess that the immediate popularity of niche periodicals for Catholic professionals came as a surprise to me, but it wasn't to Pete, who has pointed out again and again that people who love their work, who really savor the creative use of skills and tools and talents for the direct benefit of others, are almost always wonderfully receptive to the idea that their work is, as Saint Benedict observed, prayer. Benedict himself is a good case study; note the success of the organization he founded and the ways it has continued to grow and change while adhering to its original marketing mission, morphing even unto colleges and universities, which are, when you think about it, essentially factories for creating Benedictine salespeople.

Why, in the end, is *Catholic Golf Digest* such a successful entrepreneurial adventure? Beyond all the obvious reasons such as superb target research and ad recruitment, I think the answer is that both Catholicism and golf are ultimately about crazy hope. Neither makes complete sense, which may be the secret to both. The religion insists on the miracle of every moment, the imminence of immanence, the irrepressible resurrection; the sport is similar, in that every shot might be the perfect one, every round a miracle, the worst flub followed immediately by extraordinary resurrection. That mostly we bumble and snarl, whiff and shank, fail and wail, is immaterial; it is the substance of things hoped for on which we set our hearts, according to Saint Paul, and who could argue with a man who drove for such distance?

a mass

The lovely chapel where noon Mass is usually held at my university is in dry dock, having its keel repaired and generally being buffed and honed, so the noon Mass, not usually peripatetic, wandered into a classroom for awhile, and then into a tiny dormitory chapel, where it has been celebrated for a few weeks, for those of us who can find it, up the old stairs, past the soda and candy machines, and down the hall to the right, behind the door with the crucifix.

There were fourteen of us in toto yesterday, including a guide dog, who looked rapt at the whole thing and who never took his eyes off the celebrant, an immense sapling of a man who looks exactly like a young Abraham Lincoln without the hipster beard. Also there was a small child, perhaps age two, with a terrifying neck brace; she too was wonderfully attentive, never taking her eyes off the miracle in the middle of the room, which was a refreshing lesson for me, who has far too often taken his eyes off the miracles.

In a room this small there is no sitting in the back, there not being any remote regions, so we all sat essentially in a circle, and young Abe cheerfully noted in his homily that this sort of small gathering, with bread and wine and excellent stories and two miracles, surely harked back to the original meeting of the ancestral clan, which was also on an upper floor, and also featured a sinewy celebrant and twelve companions, although in our case we were luckier in that we were graced by a child, the greatest of miracles, and we were honored also by a representative from another species. Although there may well have been dogs at the Last Supper, said Abe, considering the various times in the scriptures that dogs are mentioned as scooping up bread crumbs falling from tables.

One great thing about Mass being celebrated in a crowded college dormitory is that you can hear the seething life of the hall thrumming overhead and burbling faintly through the doors and windows; not until yesterday had I enjoyed a Mass during which I heard reggae music, and the samba of washing machines, and an argument about the Satanic nature of the Los Angeles Lakers, and what sounded like a skateboard being ridden down a distant staircase at high speed. All these sounds were gentle, and did not obtrude on the music of the Mass, but somehow having the murmured soundtrack of youth in the background as we celebrated the miracles deepened the experience, added a little more of the salt and song of life to an event too often ossified as mere ritual; and what could be more beautifully human and holy than sitting over food and telling stories and insisting on miracles, in the company of a child and a dog?

At the Eucharist, when his master stood up to join the line, the guide dog stood up as well, and they both sat down simultaneously when the man returned to his pew to meditate on Christ-in-us. I think the man teaches philosophy here but I am not sure. The dog teaches grace and patience and love, perhaps.

Slipping into the rear of the chapel just before the Eucharist was a campus policeman who carefully tucked the tools of his trade into a corner of a pew before he too went up for Communion; Abe, noticing him as the end of the Communion line approached, broke the last host in two, and gave the first half to the mother of the girl with the neck brace, and the second half to the campus policeman.

It being the Feast of Saint Blaise, several people stayed after Mass to have their throats blessed, and when they were finished the mother of the girl with the neck brace asked Abe if he would ask the blessing of the Lord on her daughter, who had survived one surgery on her spine but faced another on Thursday, and Abe said sure, and cupped his enormous hands over the girl's head, as round as a small pumpkin, and did so. The girl stared at him with the most beautiful frightened green eyes I have ever seen. I noticed she only had one shoe on, her other foot wriggling happily in its pink sock, and I asked the mother if the shoe was lost, perhaps I could help hunt for it among the pews, but she said oh no, she just likes to wear the one shoe, and who am I to say no to that? She likes wearing a shoe only on her left foot, even in winter. She won't eat anything that's red, either. She has a mind of her own. Are you a priest too? Can you also bless her? I said that I was not a priest but I would absolutely hold her daughter in my heart and pray for her and maybe write a small essay so that people who read it would pray for her also, when they got to the end of the essay and found a frightened girl with one red shoe, and the mother said she would be grateful for that, so that is what I tried to do. The Mass is ended. Go in peace.

on east first street

My sister (now a Buddhist nun) having worked at the Catholic Worker St. Joseph House in New York City for a while, and my New York family being the sort of devout Catholic family that put more emphasis on doing than talking, I too showed up on First Street one day, when I was about twenty, thinking that I would perhaps magnanimously volunteer for the day, or get into a long cool intense conversation with Dorothy Day, or be instantly hired as genius-writer-in-residence, or something like that. I hadn't the faintest idea of what actually went on at St. Joseph House, you see, and I was twenty, when anything might happen except pretty much exactly that which you thought might happen; which is how and why we grow up, I suppose.

In my case I found an elderly woman standing against the brick wall, looking stern and holy, and of course I immediately assumed she was Dorothy Day, as she looked grim and spiritual.

This is Saint Joseph House? I asked.

Yup.

And you are Dorothy Day?

Who are you?

Brian Doyle.

Welcome to Saint Joseph. Hungry?

Not so much. I am here to help.

Excellent. We need a dishwasher today. Can you wash dishes? Yes ma'am. I am in college and I spend a lot of time washing dishes.

Excellent. Go in and tell them you are the dishwasher today. This I did, thinking how cool it was to be commanded in life by Dorothy Day; I mean, Dorothy Day was clearly going to be recognized as a saint eventually, and I had gotten to talk to her, so clearly some saint dust had drifted onto me, which was a good thing, because I was then twenty years old and had done some things that a little saint dust would really help out with. For a minute, there by the door, I thought maybe this was going to be an *excellent* day, saint-dust-wise, because what if I bumped into Peter Maurin, that would be a *major* load of saint dust, despite him being French, but then I remembered that this was 1977, and Peter had been deceased for nearly thirty years, so I went in to the kitchen.

I lasted about an hour as a dishwasher. You wouldn't *believe* how many dishes come through the old lunch line at Saint Joseph. You think of the words *lunch line*, and you have the vague impression of a few cheerful and colorful raggedy souls who are actually sweet and brilliant and who chaff you wittily when you say something so that you always remember how cool they were even though they were wearing boxer shorts on their heads or were talking to invisible wolverines or something. But that's not what it was like at *all*, the lunch line, which appeared to have eight million people on it that day, and they were not overly colorful and cheerful either, as they were ravenously hungry, and probably deeply concerned with where they were going to sleep, and find medical care, and survive another week, and avoid being beaten and robbed or worse. I made a couple of cheerful witty remarks and then I shut my mouth and did dishes as fast and thoroughly as I could, and when lunch slowed down I have to confess, with a little shame, even thirty-five years after that day, that I quit.

Back out front the same elderly woman was standing there looking like a cross between a cleaning lady and the queen of New York City, and she said what, you're done already?

Yes, ma'am. Worn out.

More dishes tomorrow if you want to help.

Back to college tomorrow, ma'am [a roaring lie].

Good luck with that.

Thank you.

Which college?

University of Notre Dame, ma'am.

Lots of dishes there?

Sweet Jesus yes, ma'am.

Do them well. That's a good prayer.

Yes, ma'am. An honor to meet you, ma'am.

Brian, was it?

Yes, ma'am.

My name's Eileen, she said, smiling. Pleasure to meet you too. Remember: doing the dishes well, that's a real good prayer.

And the thing is, despite my initial disappointment that Eileen was not Dorothy Day, I never forgot her advice, which was as fine a spiritual piece of advice as I ever got, and over the years I came to realize that I had had the great fortune to meet a lady named Eileen, who was, of course, a saint. It turns out that everyone either is a saint or can still be one; a lesson I started to learn on East First Street, many years ago.

piléir

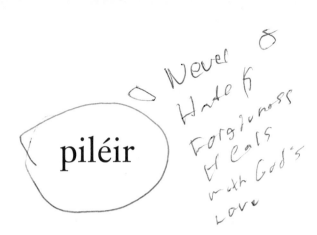

Never Hate
Forgiveness
Heals
with God's
Love

One night I was sitting with a friend whose people had fled County Donegal many years ago; more properly we were *asked* to leave, said my friend; or more properly still we were *made* to leave, by the bailiffs; most properly, if we are using exact words, we were evicted, and had to live in the wet lanes and fields, and the few of my people who did not starve to death, or die of the fever, made their way onto boats, hiding in the stench of scuppers and stink of holds, and those who did not die at sea survived in the new lands, and eventually produced me. But we remember, we remember. For example, here is a story you should know.

One morning in Donegal, during the time when the penal laws are in effect and Catholics are forbidden to assemble for Mass, a farmer herds his four black cows into a corral, along with one white one. This is a sign to his fellow Catholics as to where Mass will be held at noon; this sign of four and one means in a particular hedge under a hill. The people casually drift away from their work before noon and assemble silently around a rock where the Mass will be celebrated. The priest is a fellow age forty. He gets halfway through the Mass, but just as he elevates the host at the apex of the Mass, just as he lifts it to accept and accomplish the miracle, he is drilled between the eyes with a bullet from a British soldier on the hill. The priest falls down dead and the host flutters into the mud. The usual uproar then ensues

and several men are arrested and the priest is buried in a pau-
per's grave.

The soldier is a man age forty also, with a young son about
age ten. The soldier finishes his year of duty in Ireland and goes
home to Bristol. His son is a scholarly lad and goes to university and then into the ministry. At age thirty the boy is a curate,
with all his future smiling before him, and there are many who
think he will be Archbishop of Canterbury before too long. But
something happens to the boy and he grows more and more
interested in how Anglicanism grew from Catholicism. This is a
dangerous road and his superiors frown upon his inquiries, but
he persists. By the time he is thirty-five he makes the break, and
converts to Catholicism; five years later he is a Catholic priest, to
the immense dismay of his father.

One night the father, terribly frustrated and angry, loses his
temper, and tells his son something he has never confessed to
a soul, not even to his late wife, the boy's mother: that he
shot and killed a priest just as the priest was about to celebrate
the instant when the Catholics believe the very essence of the
Creator incomprehensibly enters a scrap of bread held high in
the air. The son covers his face with his hands as the father,
shouting, says he never regretted that shot for an instant, and
that he never made such a fine shot before or since, and that the
priest and his fellow conspirators got what they deserved, just
that, only that, exactly that.

A month later the son, having researched the annals of the
constabulary for the incident, and visited the village, and asked
its oldsters where hedge Masses were held in the dark days, finds
the rock under the hill, and gathers the villagers one morning,
and finishes the Mass that was interrupted thirty years before
by a bullet. When Mass is over, he and the villagers bury an

unconsecrated host and a bullet, *piléir*, in the earth by the rock, and then they all trail along back to the village. Now that is a story you should know, said my friend, and you tell it yourself, when you can, and the more people who know it, the fewer bullets there will be, perhaps.

john's last
mass

His voice shivered only once, at the very end, when he finished Mass with a line he'd spoken every Sunday for ten years: *Most of all, be kind—it is a sure sign of God's presence and love.*

But he composed himself, and stepped down from the altar and waited for the readers and Eucharistic ministers, and then they all walked singing down the aisle, John high-fiving small children along the way, and that was the last minute of his last Mass.

But it wasn't really the end. He stood by the door as the entire congregation walked past and people hugged him and handed him flowers and such, and then he wandered out into the parking lot, leaning on car doors and laughing and talking, and then he and a kid threw a tennis ball for his dog Sadie for a while, and then someone gave him a ride to the picnic in his honor, which went on all afternoon, with excellent beer and the terrific harmonica player who sometimes showed up to play Sunday morning but more often didn't; and finally in the early evening, John's last Mass did end.

Someone gave him a ride home in the gathering darkness.

He'd been pastor for ten years—busy years too, as he was also chaplain at the big public hospital up the road, with all the death and despair of that job, but it was rewarding work too, he said;

work that helps people come back to God occasionally, and eases their hearts in awful times. And there was all the regular work of a parish: sacraments and Masses and meetings and shuttling food to the homeless shelter and cutting the grass and figuring out what to do about the leaky roof.

Under his eye, the parish hummed with a verve and humor and easy grace that had a great deal to do with John but didn't revolve around him, for he was careful never to be a star but only a celebrant, his favorite word. But his personality infused the place, relaxed it, focused it. Joining the parish during John's tenure, for example, was pretty straightforward: You called him up and he'd say, You want to be a member of the parish? You're a member of the parish. See you Sunday.

His tenure ended finally, as things do, and John was transferred, but before he left he said one last Mass, which was crammed to the gills.

He gave a State of the Parish speech near the end, and he apologized for talking at length, but he felt responsible to account for his time, and he had a few things to say personally, so he said them.

He went over the finances, which were way in the black, and he said that he'd contracted for a new roof, and he said that without casting aspersions he felt that when he came ten years ago the parish was rudderless, and that wasn't the case anymore, and it wasn't his doing but ours, which we knew wasn't wholly true, but we all savored the compliment.

He said that we had together built a vibrant and generous clan here on the hill, and that we owed it to the next guy to give him a chance, and we owed it to ourselves to stay together, not to let parish politics break up what we had made. *Remember*, he said, *there is no door that love will not open, no sin it will not redeem.*

He said, his voice quivering badly now, that he loved being a priest, and that he had never loved it so much, with such delight and peace, as he had in these years with these people in this church.

Then he was silent for a minute and so was everyone else.

Then he said *Most of all, be kind—it is a sure sign of God's presence and love*, and he blessed everyone, and pretty much all the adults were weeping by now but not the children, because they knew that this line meant the end of Mass, and then the last song was supposed to begin but the guitarist said *We can't let Father John leave without applause, can we?* and there was a sea of applause which went on and on and on.

Finally the band played the last song and John stepped down from the altar and walked singing down the aisle, and that was the end.

But we remember.

stunning and lovely

When I was a child, many years ago, at a parish named for a saint famous for hearing confessions for eighteen hours at a pop, my life was graced by Dominican nuns, some of whom had ropy forearms like stevedores, and by Franciscan monks, all of whom seemed to have knotted feet made from tree roots, and once by a Jesuit, who looked so forbiddingly intelligent that we school-children scattered like sparrows when he passed silently through the schoolyard, because rumor had it that Jesuits had laser eyes and could kill sparrows by staring at them hard, but most of us thought this was silly, although all of us flittered away from the Jesuit right quick.

Thus I was introduced, when young, to the different flavors of Catholic charism: the Order of Preachers in their brilliant whites, the Order of Friars Minor in their quiet browns, and the brainy blackrobed intensity of the Society of Jesus, not to men-tion the steady priests of the Archdiocese of New York, who gen-erally dressed like dentists on golf outings when they weren't in uniform. The religious orders, it seemed to us boys, were not unlike the military, with Regular Army personnel carrying most of the daily duty and specialists coming in for specific tasks—the Franciscans to conduct retreats, the Jesuit for astrophysics semi-nars or other such incomprehensible rites, the burly Dominican sisters to haul our faltering mental machinery into the shop for heroic renovation and repair. Not until I got to college, where I encountered the cheerful men of the Congregation of Holy Cross and their nutty insistence that I could learn as much or more outside the classroom than in it, and to middle age, when I became absorbed by the Sisters of the Holy Names of Jesus and Mary and their nutty insistence that missionary work was as crucial Here as There, did I begin to pay close attention to the often-infinitesimal but riveting distinctions among the Catholic orders.

In a real sense the military model holds water still, for it seems to me that every Catholic order is an agent of the same brave hope and crazy conviction, that life defeats death, hope defeats despair, light defeats dark; they're all on the same team, as it were, and all of them affiliated with colleges and universities use the same bland words: active faith, service as prayer, spiritual search, etc. Yet each comes at the mountain of problems along a slightly different path. Work and prayer, work *is* prayer, say the Benedictines, insisting that actions are more eloquent than words. Epiphany is *everywhere* available, say the Holy Cross men and women, and an education of the heart is as crucial as that of the mind. In the beginning was the Word, say the Order of Preachers, and the Word *is* God, and we will speak the Word wide. We are all brothers and sisters in the Love, say the Franciscans, who insist on living the gospel, not just analyzing it—if *necessary* use words, as their entertaining founder noted. Go thou to *the most difficult and extreme fields*, said Pope Paul VI to the Jesuits, and away they still go, agents of love into the jungles of despair, examples to their students of quiet courage changing the world. And there are as many more examples as there are Catholic orders in higher education; but for all the thrashing about that we poor badgers in their public relations offices must do, trying to shout the differences among them so as to secure market share, I confess here that in our hearts we are thrilled that the differences are so tiny—shimmers of sunlight, really. Every color in the rainbow wears a different jacket, but the colors together compose something stunning and lovely beyond words, yes?

the baptismee

Went to a baptism the other day, in a lovely old empty echoing church, on one of those crisp afternoons when the sun comes in through the old mullioned windows so powerfully it looks like glowing bronze wood.

I am the baptismer, said the tall priest with a smile, and this is our baptismee, in the lovely white frilly dress. His name is Vincent, as you know.

The baptismee was a couple of months old and just past the stage where infants all look like Yoda. The baptismee, in fact, was just hitting his first serious growth spurt, what with all his magic mother's milk, and it seemed like all of his first growth had gone to his head, for his head was tremendous, and his eyes, wide open in amazement at the light coming through the windows, looked to be the size of baseballs, from where I was standing in the back.

That kid needs a zip code for his head, said the man next to me, quietly.

The godparents hustled up to the altar and the young godfather, niggling at what was probably the first necktie he had worn since his First Communion, said *We do!* when the priest said hello, which got a general laugh.

The priest buckled down to business but he did so with such an easy grace that I was moved and proud of what a great priest can do. He managed to get in a good deal of church history and custom and belief about why we were baptizing this new boy, while never being in the least ponderous or pompous or officious about it. He was relaxed and funny. He turned ritual into celebration. He asked everyone to come on up on the altar for heaven's sake and touch the boy, give him your blessing, pray for him with your fingers for a moment, because Christ was skin and bone like us, remember, and then he asked all children to stay gathered closely around the baptismee, because it would relax the boy to have his fellow small tribe around him, and also if Vincent squirmed and plummeted, you young folks have lightning reflexes, so if he dives for the floor, catch him like a big baseball, which also got a general laugh.

That kid will have a head like a suitcase if he keeps growing at this rate, said the man next to me.

Some children, when you baptize them, said the priest, they pee like horses, so you probably want to stand back a little, just in case, but Vincent, I note, is not wailing or asleep, which gives me hope that he will be a continental boy, so to speak. He must have *excellent* parents.

Why is the baby wearing a dress if he is a boy? said a small girl suddenly, which got another laugh.

As the priest anointed the baptismee with oil, the baby squirmed a little and the priest said, well, we were aiming for a cross there on his head, and I think we got closer to a Star of David, but Christ was Jewish, you remember, so we will also apparently be honoring our parent stock this afternoon. We could try to anoint Vincent again but I think we got close enough the first time for it to count, don't you?

The godparents made the usual promises, and the parents made sure to give the boy the name they had agreed to give him when they met him face-to-face for the first time, and the priest noted that Vincent was a cool name because there were excellent saints named Vincent and the boy would have a sort of posse or entourage among saintly men of that name, which couldn't hurt as he grew into his glorious and holy lifetime.

That kid has a head bigger than a basketball, said the man next to me, who turned out to be the boy's grandfather, a Navy veteran who had spent twenty years in submarines and once baptized a child on a beach in Vietnam for reasons he did not wish to explain at length in the church although he said perhaps later over a beer.

When the baptism was complete, the priest held out the baptismee like a championship trophy and we all reached out and touched him again, and while he did indeed have a head like a pumpkin, it was his broad smile that stays with me. He looked really pleased and proud, even with a sort of Cross of David on his head, and you could see his feet kicking happily against the bottom of his frilly white dress. Then the priest gave Vincent back to his parents and everyone shook hands and there were a few minutes of milling and laughing and then everyone repaired back to the house for a beer. On the way to the house I thought about how our church is these little sweet honest funny moments more than it is everything else, and how I love that, and how these little sweet honest funny moments are so holy I cannot easily find words for them, which is why we share stories, which is what we just did. Amen.

a halting
holiness

Why was the late Polish playwright Karol Wojtyla indeed a superb pope, and one of the great religious leaders of modern times?

For all the reasons you would expect, of course, the feats that will echo for centuries: his creative genius for image and symbol, his courage and humor surviving an assassination attempt, the brave humility that led him to bow in prayer at Jerusalem's Wailing Wall and kneel in apology for two millennia of Catholic sins, the capacious imagination and energy that helped free Poland and shatter the Iron Curtain, his clear voice against war, his relentless insistence that life was a holy gift, even the enormous physical courage he evinced in recent years as he deliberately remained a public figure as his body failed—I think in order to show the world that pain and death are not our masters, that grace under duress is a form of ferocious prayer, that the spirit outlives the body.

But there is a deeper and truer reason to say that this man was wonderfully Christlike, was a spiritual exemplar of rare wattage, and paradoxically that reason is what he did badly—his thousand mistakes, his astounding stubbornness, the dense thicket of contradictions that defined his papacy as much or more than the astounding parade of his accomplishments.

For this was also the man who choked off liberation theology in Latin America when it might have toppled that haunted continent's web of corrupt governments, even as he sang and celebrated it in Europe. This was the man who presided over a church revealed worldwide to be riven with the rapes of children. This was a man who time and time again dismissed women—more than half the billion members of his church!—from any serious role and voice in the ancient corporation. This was the man who spoke warmly of the innate brotherhood of Christianity's many sects but did little practically to bind ancient rifts.

It seems to me that the worst thing that could happen to the legacy of John Paul II, now that his spirit is with the Light he believed in with all his might, is to reduce him to immediate sainthood. Saintly he was, of course, and he may well have been as great a leader, in his way, as the greatest pope I have seen in my lifetime, tiny cheerful John XXIII, who had the courage in 1965 to take the Church he loved by its ancient hoary arrogant throat and shake it until the dust and hubris fell like snow.

But John Paul's greatest accomplishment, I believe, is that he was so patently and daily and persistently Us: feat and flaw, virtue and vice, brilliance and blindness. This man, this priest, this servant of the faithful, evinced, on the world stage, for nearly twenty-seven years, the essence of the Catholic faith: the crazy hope that we are capable of complete mercy and grace and courage and humility and generosity, that we are more than mammal, that against all the daily evidence of our creative cupidity and predilection for violence is the constant possibility of love, in all its billion forms. The Catholic Church was created (largely by Saint Paul, the greatest public relations man in history) to carry that mad message to the ends of the earth, and despite all its flaws and flops over these twenty centuries, the Church is still in business, and still graced by such remarkable people as Dorothy Day and Thomas Merton, Cardinals Joseph Bernadin and Carlo Martini, Oscar Romero and Cesar Chavez, Flannery O'Connor and Mother Teresa of Calcutta. And John Paul II.

He did not do everything well; he did some things very poorly indeed, or did not do them at all. Yet at the same time he was a man of stunning presence and charisma, a corporate leader of wonderful creativity, a figure of light and hope for many millions of people—especially, and perhaps most crucially to the century he leaves behind, young people. The same Church recently revealed to have not only allowed but hidden thousands of rapes also has attracted many thousands of young converts around the world, drawn to the message of hope by the grinning man in white robes. That is remarkable and perhaps this pope's most enduring legacy.

Like the gaunt devout Jew Yeshuah ben Joseph, whom we know as Jesus the Christ, who also was a human being and so utterly liable to foible (remember that he sassed his parents, lost his temper in the temple courtyard, and was often curt and testy with his posse), the late pope was no stranger to muddle and stumble; but he strove with amazing energy and constancy to connect to people and share his deepest conviction, that we are carved of holy stuff, and, as Saint Paul said, there is Christ in each of us.

May he rest in peace, Karol Wojtyla, and be remembered with admiration and respect and prayers in our mouths; and may he be remembered best not for what he did well, but for the courage and grace with which he kept trying to rise to mercy and humility. The message of the Christ, ultimately, is not a mere church;

it is an idea, a wild crazy paradoxical illogical unreasonable idea, the nutty idea that love defeats murder, life defeats death, hope defeats despair, the soul supersedes time. This pope devoted his life to that idea, and the seed of his greatness, it seems to me, is that his very public successes and failures, on a worldwide stage, have spread the idea to billions of people. So the man who was an actor before he accepted another job offer may well have been the greatest performer of our time—a thought that amuses him, I hope, in the unimaginable new country where he now resides.

rise up, my love

The university's chapel again undergoing renovations having to do with bringing light to corners dim and musty since Jesus was a teenager, the noon Mass is again peripatetic, and today it was celebrated in an old classroom. All nine of us sat under an immense wall map of Rome "in the time of the pharaohs," as the young woman next to me informed me helpfully.

To the south there was an oil portrait of a brooding benefactor and a bulletin board festooned with class assignments and stern remonstrations; west was Rome, in all its eternal glory; east was a stack of folding chairs, in case of a miraculous surge of celebrants; and north, behind the makeshift altar and the dapper Father Celebrant, was a huge thermostat, as big as a hat, and two tremendous windows facing the university's central quadrangle. The students being gone for Christmas break, only surly jays and ebullient crows flitted by during Mass that I noticed, although one time there was a sudden flurry in the grass, which may have been a hawk or a grapple of squirrels.

The first reading is from the Song of Songs, *my beloved spake, and said unto me, rise up, my love, my fair one, and come away,* and miraculously my soul did leap, like a roe or a young hart, for reasons I do not understand, and realize I will never understand, and no longer care to understand; it's not the words, lovely as

they are, read with passion as they are, but some inchoate inartic-
ulate knowledge that there *is* a One who loveth me, and looketh
forth, and showeth Himself through the lattices, and driveth the
flowers and the turtles, the birds and the figs, the foxes and the
vines; and though He standeth behind a wall, and is hidden in
the clefts of the rocks, and the secret places of the stairs, I *do* see
His countenance, and hear His voice, in every blessed bruised
moment, if my eyes and ears are open—even moments like this
one, when the skies are moist and gray, and it is November in
my soul, and my worries do crest as though they were floods in
the blood, and my fears for those I love who are ill and dark do
be legion.

The second reading is from Luke, *and when Elisabeth heard
the salutation of Mary, the babe leaped in her womb; and Elisabeth
was filled with the spirit, and spake out with a loud voice, and said,
as soon as the voice of thy salutation sounded in mine ears, the babe
leaped in my womb for joy!* and again my heart leapt, against all
sense and reason. It's just a story, isn't it? It's just a story. It might
well be fiction. It might well be a biblical editorial committee's
way to foreshadow the arrival of the One in flesh like mine,
only younger and browner. It might be utterly and egregiously
untrue, a dream, a lie from tip to toe. Yet my soul did leap for
joy, and I too blessed the womb that carried that Child, and I
too shuffled silently and moved toward the thermostat and the
tremendous windows to eat the bread that is not bread; and having eaten it I was changed, in subtle ways I do not understand.

We do not often admit that the essence of what we say and
think and believe is utterly nonsensical, in every way, from the
belief that there is a Lover who showeth Himself through the lattices, to the bread that is not bread. But almost every time I am
soaked in the waters of the Mass, especially when it is celebrated

not in glorious cathedrals but in musty basements and dusty classrooms, on dining room tables and rickety boards propped on sawhorses, my soul doth leap, and a deep thirst is slaked in some way I do not understand, and I shuffle out cleaner, quieter, happier. I cannot tell you how this is so, and all the words I use are weak. Yet it happens to me, and it has happened to you. I do not know how this sweet crucial thing can happen, or what it means, or how to explain it. But the very fact that it is there for us, possible, waiting, daily, all over the world, in every language, no matter how many people have tried to kill and forbid it, is an extraordinary thing that we should occasionally, with something like awe, sing aloud; and so, this afternoon, I do.

the letter

He rose before six that morning, the same as usual, and donned his sweatshirt, and went for a jog—three miles now, in a slight concession to age, rather than four. Then a shower and coffee and an hour of private prayer in his home chapel. It was Ash Wednesday. A light day for appointments, he says—everyone assumes you're in church all day, which you are not, although I was celebrating a Mass at noon at the chancery and the Mass at five in the cathedral.

It was also his seventy-fifth birthday. An archbishop of the Holy Roman Catholic Church, by canon law, must tender his resignation, by letter, to His Holiness the Pope by the close of business on his seventy-fifth birthday. The letter must be post-marked that day. The mail is picked up at four in the after-noon at the chancery on Burnside Street. So His Excellency John George Vlazny, tenth archbishop of Portland, Oregon, the second-oldest archdiocese in America (behind only Baltimore), had some seven hours, after his arrival in his office on Burn-side Street at nine in the morning on Ash Wednesday, to write the letter that would close his career as not only Oregon's pas-tor, but first among the Catholic bishops of Oregon, Idaho, and Montana.

I figured I would tackle it as soon as I got settled in the office, he says. No sense putting it off. No, I didn't worry about what to say. I knew what I was *supposed* to say, but I also knew what

I *wanted* to say. I dictated the letter, as I usually do. I told the Holy Father that I was filled with the deepest appreciation for having received the call to be a bishop three times from His Holiness John Paul the Second, and that I was offering my resignation, and that I would await further information. The letter goes to the papal nuncio in Washington, and then he reports my resignation to the Congregatio pro Episcopis, the Congregation for Bishops, in the Vatican. In turn they report my news to His Holiness, and then the process starts. I am eventually asked for the *terna*, three men I think would be excellent candidates to succeed me. The three names can be anyone in the world—I could even suggest *you*, although if the Holy Father chooses you, which he can, we would have to see about your ordination.

I wasn't sad or regretful, no. To be honest there was almost a little glee, after twenty-nine years as a bishop. When I finished dictating the letter, I left the tape in a box by the door. My assistant Roseanne retrieved it. Our habit is that she types up letters and gives them to me to look over and sign. In this case she waited until the afternoon to get to it.

I stared at the tape all morning but I just couldn't do it, she says. I just couldn't bring myself to do it. I knew that I should but I just couldn't. Finally after lunch he said, I think you better get that letter done, Roseanne, so I did. I gave it to him at about two o'clock. He made some tinkers and I made him a clean copy, and he signed that and gave it back to me. We didn't say anything. I put it in the envelope and stamped it. I remember that the stamp had a ship on it. I walked it down to the mailroom. Outgoing mail goes in a large white bin. A postman comes for the bin. Our mail goes to the main city post office on Hoyt Street. The letter goes to Washington, and then I think it goes into the papal nuncio's diplomatic pouch for transmission to Rome.

You know what I would like to do when I am retired? says the archbishop. I'd like to sit by the Sea of Galilee for a couple of months. Or maybe in the hills of Assisi. Just sit quietly and think and pray. It's been a long road from being Johnny Vlazny in the streets of Chicago to that letter. Fifty years as a priest, thirty as a bishop. Then I'd like to come home to Portland and just be on call. Visit schools, retreats, maybe teach a little. The archdiocese is in good health now. We're out of bankruptcy, no parishes closed, the schools are all protected. The parishes are independent. I am a member of 150 parish corporations, you know. Vocations are up, Hispanics are better served, our children are protected against heinous crimes. We're in good shape. I know that my time will always be remembered for the scandal and the bankruptcy. I don't like that, but I know how history will read.

Your Excellency, I say, there are an awful lot of people who think your honesty and humility and integrity dealing with crimes not committed on your watch is what will be remembered. You said you would protect our children, and be responsible to victims, and never lie, and you kept your promises, when many other men did not.

There was a moment, says the archbishop suddenly, when I was about to sign off on the bankruptcy, which would be the first ever in the American church, but which I felt we must do, to be fair to all victims and to protect parishes and schools from closure, and I hesitated for a moment, thinking that this might well get me fired by Rome; but then I realized that if you are not willing to be fired, you are not doing your job. I suppose I would like to be remembered as a man who did his job with all his heart. I never wanted to be an authority. I only wanted to be a good priest, and a good man, and a teacher of the greatest lesson I know.

Right about then the archbishop's next appointment is announced and we shake hands and I look around his office, the last time I will ever see him here, and I note three things in particular: a shepherd's crook, carved for him by a parishioner; a walking-stick owned by a nineteenth-century predecessor archbishop; and a drawing by a child. This last is positioned so that he can see it all day, every day.

the late
mr. bin laden:
a note

And what could anyone add to the ocean of comment and opinion and conclusion and musing and snarling and vengeful remarks published and shouted about the recent death of Mr. O. bin Laden, late of Abbottabad, Pakistan, shot to death in his bedroom, perhaps with his television remote in his hand, perhaps moments after he finished coloring his beard black again for a video production scheduled for the morning? Not much, especially in my case, after nearly ten years of quiet rage that he murdered three of my friends on September 11, cackling over their deaths, a cackle I will never forget as long as I live. And yet, and yet, I find myself thinking how very sad; not his death, in which the bullets he had so often assigned to others found him at last, but his life, wasted on a foolish and murderous idea, causing such epic wreckage, and perhaps in the end doing far more damage to his beloved religion than anyone else in its long and often admirable history.

I say this as a Catholic man, well aware that my religion tried bin Laden's idea and found it a roaring failure, responsible for uncountable deaths of innocent souls; we call our collective terrorism campaign the Crusades, and even the most rabid among Catholics today cannot say with a straight face that our attacks on the infidel succeeded in anything except gaining the Church a well-deserved reputation for militant murder. And from those bloody years the Church sensibly retreated back mostly to a business model, spending the next seven hundred years as one of the largest, richest, most influential, riveting, and troubled corporations in human history. Catholic nations continued to send agents to murder and rob the pagans of the New World, certainly, but rather than murder other established religions we sought to outpopulate them, ignore them, negotiate complex truces, or, as we did recently with the Anglicans, offer them readmission to the mother ship from which years ago they embarked, in their case because of the sexual politics of kings, one of the great human spectator sports. In a real sense, after the Crusades finally petered to their ignominious end, we matured as a religion; we realized that the sword was the worst of persuasive devices, and we turned to other hinges of history, some brilliant, like the public relations geniuses Mother Teresa of India, Karol Wojtyła of Poland, Dorothy Day of Brooklyn, and the elementary school system on which much of modern Catholicism was built. Today, long centuries after we waged holy war against people who called God other names than we did, there are a billion Catholics in the world, and two billion followers of the devout Jew Yeshuah ben Joseph.

It was the fervent dream of the late Mr. bin Laden that an epic war arise between the nearly two billion followers of Muhammad ibn Abdullāh, blessed be his name, and the followers of Yeshuah ben Joseph, blessed be his name. This fiery dream, born in 1998 with the murder of Kenyan and Tanzanian innocents, consumed twenty years of what must have been a very bright intellect, an often-attested-to personal charisma, and a mountainous personal

Clans &
Tribes

fatherness: a note

As Father's Day hoves into view like a tiny bird that you are vaguely aware of but do not acknowledge with more than a new necktie or a hurriedly scrawled card for the old goat, I sit in the shaggy wilderness of the yard, listening to the tiny birds and contemplating fatherhood, fatherness, fatheritude. My own fatherhood, a state I sought with many prayers and pleadings twenty years ago, has turned out to be exhausting and exhilarating in nearly the same proportions, although immeasurable joy is winning by a nose at the moment, the children having emerged recently from teenage snarlery like butterflies from chrysalii. My father's fatherhood, a state in which he has lived with remarkable grace and patience for sixty-SEVEN years, continues as lively and nutritious as an ocean, though he is now headlong into his nineties and sets a new world record for longest-lived male in the history of our clan every morning when he wakes—a record he likes to chirp about to my mom, who rolls her eyes.

But it is the Father of All That Is whom I think about most this morning, in the garden, and it is He whom I wish to talk about with you, as the tiny birds flit by faster than we can see. And this morning I use the word *Father* with an easy conscience; for all that I understand and empathize with the final foolishness of assigning mere gender to That which said *I Am Who Am* from the burning bush, for all that I bow to those who sigh at the words He and Him when we speak of *I Am Who Am*, for all that I myself am often the first to say we are fools and charlatans to say we know anything surely of the Unimaginable One except what many of us believe to be clear and inarguable messages delivered through a gaunt Jewish man many years ago, today I consider His Fatherhood, for to think of the Shining One as a father is a revelatory window into the thrilling mystery of the gift we have been given—a gift we take for granted, much like we take fathers for granted, except on the day we deluge them with ties and cards.

Willful, impatient, testy, demanding, capricious, He is all of those things, or so our forebears thought; cf. the Old Testament. Yet He also gave us everything we have, everything we could ever imagine we wanted, everything we cannot even imagine yet that we would ever need or want or be awed by, in its beauty and miraculous profligacy. Is it not the story of our sciences that now, after so many years of hard work, we know only a drop of the endless ocean of creation?

Subject to choosing favorites; subject to fits of titanic temper; subject to waves of disgust and despair—we have many stories of these things in the annals of the voice from the bush. Yet He died for us, as every decent father would without hesitation die for his children, without a second thought, without even the slight calculation of their opening future against his narrowing one. No, if what we believe of the Son is true, then the Son and the Father are the same being, Who gave us not only a universe extraordinary beyond our ken, but finally Himself, in a mysterious Eucharist, a sacrifice that never ends, a gift repeated every day all over the world He left behind in that skin in that century in that desert, bloody then and bloody now, the poor haunted land.

As the late great Catholic writer Andre Dubus said, *if I could give my children my body to eat, again and again without losing it, my body like the loaves and fishes going endlessly into mouths and stomachs, I would do it*, and of course you would too, that is what fathers do, they give themselves away, willingly, happily, and that is what the Eucharist is, the Father giving us Himself every day . . .

Our own three children are nearly grown now, and I sit often in the garden amid the tiny birds and contemplate that which I have done well and that which I have done not so well. As best I could, I gave our children peace and good food, light and clean air, education and clean water, a set of expectations to exceed and a foundation of values and ideas from which to leap. By luck and prayer their mother and father stayed married and so gave their children a brace of loving parents, an example of interested commitment, a balance of older personalities and flavors and genders; and so our children are by many measures rich beyond calculation; they have never starved, been raped, been shot at, scrabbled for shelter, been utterly alone without kith or kin. And now one is away at university and soon the others, and a crucial phase of my fatherhood will have passed, though I know full well, from watching my own father's deft work closely, that fatherhood never ends, and I will worry about them forever, and I will stash small amounts of cash for their sudden plaintive calls, and for all that I sing their independence and the way they will create extraordinary mature selves from the tall seeds they are now, I know I will mourn their absence, and growl when they are lazy and selfish, and very probably continue to be slightly too hard on them, because I love them in ways I cannot explain, and I want the world for them.

Which is what the Father wants for us, do you see? And He cannot bring that world to full flower, to fruition, to final epic brilliance, without His children. I believe this means *all* His children, every being there is and has been, of every species, all sparked by His breath, all set alight by His love; but yes, I believe there is a special duty and responsibility for my species, and that is perhaps why evolution has brought us to this trembling pass.

Perhaps the Father needs *us* for His dreams and visions to be fulfilled. Perhaps that is why we were chosen as His people, above all the other species; not for dominion or domination, not to foul and ruin creation, but to grow finally to be like Him, to achieve our best selves, to complete the dream He had for us; to grow fully into the Christ who is a seed in every heart. Perhaps that is why He came into this world in the most unlikely of human skins, that of a poor man in a village at the edge of an empire, and why that young man gave His life for all of ours; because that is what fathers do. They give away their lives to their children, because they love their children, and they wish their children to be greater and sweeter and happier and holier than they were, and they would do anything to give their children a world of joy and peace and water and light and laughter and mercy; and that is what He did, do you see? That is what He did for us, because He is our Father, and in ways we can never know or imagine He sees us, and prays that we will rise, and rages that he cannot force us to His will, and wishes more than anything perhaps to sing our glory, to celebrate the day when we become as we were meant to be, imagined to be, dreamed to be, a species that has matured past violence and greed and swims in light and laughter as if we were designed for them; as perhaps we were, perhaps we were.

I sit in the garden, the tiny birds whizzing and whirring, and think of my gracious brave father, who fought in not one but two wars and is the most articulate man on earth about the stupidity of war; and while I have often thought that my great ambition as a man and a father is to be half the man and father my dad is, I also realize that Fathers' Day is a superb day to dream of being a step closer to the father that the Father is. That is what we are called to do, I think; male and female, young and old. I am only reminding us. If we love as He loves us, there will come a day when our brilliance has defeated our darkness, and that will be a day of glory and song. In a very real sense that will be the greatest Father's Day there ever was.

the brilliantine
coattails of
lust

I remember walking home from grade school with my sister and brother on the day that my class had started discussion of the Sacrament of First Confession, and Proper Respect and Reverence for the Sacrament by Which Our Souls are Cleansed. It had been a day of capital letters like that, and stern and severe expectations, and I was sore afraid and weary.

Once home I performed the usual rituals of eating everything I could get my hands on before my many brothers did, and wrestling with one brother, and threatening assault and mayhem on the youngest for sheer entertainment, before our sister, who would later become a nun in a monastery, told us, not for the first time either, that if we did not stop threatening the youngest she would snap our fingers like twigs, which she was fully capable of doing, being one of those wiry strong young women with a jab like you wouldn't believe. Then it was time for dinner.

After dinner I did my homework, and then I set to the particular project assigned to us by Sister Marie for that night: choose one older sister or brother who has been cleansed by the Sacrament of First Confession, and open discussion of the implications of the same for you, writing at least one page of notes on your conversation, which will be Reviewed Tomorrow in Class, and for *this* assignment there are no excuses on this green earth that will get you out of it, not hungry dogs nor the deaths of remote aunts, not bad weather nor awful illness. If you are not in class tomorrow with your assignment in hand, written in such a manner that I can actually read it, you will not proceed with Preparation for the Sacrament of First Confession, and God help the boy or girl in my class who does not so proceed. It would be better that you were saddled by a millstone and thrown into the stormy sea.

My sister was busy thrashing a brother, so I approached my oldest brother, who not only had survived the Sacrament of First Confession, but had been Confirmed in Christ, and was now in Catholic High School, and doing so well academically that there was a chance, a whisper of a chance to be sure but oh how alluring that whisper was, that he might, if all went well and prayers were answered and our father robbed a series of banks, be accepted by, and subsequently enroll at, the University of Notre Dame, where the Madonna lived when She came to America. My oldest brother, usually not especially helpful with homework assignments, given that he had to study a thousand hours a day to have a chance at Notre Dame, was this evening for some reason in a cheerful mood, and he readily assented to assist me in this demanding task. He suggested, with as much solicitous kindness as I can ever remember from those years, that he propose some lines of inquiry, and I take careful notes, so that as I prepared for the Sacrament of First Confession I would have a running head start on the kind of sins that the priest was looking for, and not waste anyone's time in the box, time being a precious thing, of course.

This seemed sensible to me, and anyway I was so much younger than he was and I so worshipped the ground he walked on that if he had suggested I sew a skunk costume and sing Perry Como songs backwards in confession I would have leapt at the idea, so I got my notebook and prepared to take down, as meticulously as possible, his suggestions.

Start by being honest about lust, he said. Write that down. Admit lustful intentions right away. *Then* go to theft and battery. The priest will still be rattled by your opening move and he won't be quite as horrified by the sins that ride on the brilliantine coattails of lust. Are you writing this down? *Brilliantine*—I'll spell it for you. Then stall with the traditional dishonoring of your mother and father, which God knows is true. Then slip in lust again; you'll have lulled him for a moment with the cliché. Choose a girl you have a humiliating crush on and say how you daydream about her full and delicious lips, not unlike a perfectly ripe pear, and just as inviting to bite. Write that down.

But I don't have a crush, I said. What's a crush?

Never mind, he said. Now here I suggest you throw a haymaker. Make his life interesting. The poor man, inundated by the simple sins of children for hours at a time. Give him something to remember. Tell him you punched a cardinal in the nose once and not by accident. You can't remember *which* cardinal, but you got your feet set and really nailed the guy, small as you are, and you would do it again in a heartbeat. Don't go into detail, it'll just confuse him, and for God's sake *don't* lie and say something like the cardinal was at our house for dinner. It's a mistake to lie in confession, because the priest is a wily old goat and he remembers everything. He's *trained*. Whereas you are *not* trained and he will catch you in a conundrum and you'll have to go to prison and Mom will be mad. *Conundrum*—it's spelled like it sounds. Sound it out slowly. This is your home-work, not mine.

By now I had almost a whole page of notes, and my brother leaned back and thought for a moment about how to end it exactly right. I don't think I had ever been so grateful to him as I was that moment; for him to take a few precious moments out of his own homework time to help me, when I didn't have a mosquito's chance in winter of being accepted or enrolling at the University of Notre Dame, was just amazing to me.

You'll only have a minute or two left by this point, said my brother, leaning in companionably and checking my handwriting. I'd go back to lust, just to get him off balance again, and then end with something out of left field. Tell him, as qui-etly as possible—lower your voice, you know, and deepen it a little, like you are really ashamed and embarrassed—that you have decided to be a Lutheran. Leave the word hanging there luridly in the air, you know what I mean? Then say your Act of Contrition as fast as you possibly can and get out of there before he can stick his head out of the box and see who you are. Under-stand? If he sees you, it's prison for sure, and Mom will be mad.

This completed my page perfectly, and I marveled at how he knew exactly when to stop helping me with my homework, and he went back to his own homework for Catholic High School, and I made a clean copy of the notes he had given me, mak-ing sure that every word was written as clear as I could possibly write. Then I wrote *Jesus Mary Joseph* on the top of my paper, and signed my name, and put the assignment carefully in my binder, and went to bed.

I don't think I ever looked forward to school more than I did that night, for I knew full well that I had completed the assign-ment in a way that no boy before me ever had, and Sister Marie would find a paper filled with marvels on her desk in the morning, and very probably neither she nor I would ever forget the instant when she looked up, with her shining young face prettier than Julie Andrews or any other saint who ever was, and found me sitting in the fifth seat in the first row, beaming.

his epic head

My late brother Kevin had a whopper of a head, so big you could plant crops on it or lease sections for grazing; it started out as a really long head when he was a teenager, seemingly several inches longer than wide, but over the years somehow it lost some long and gained some wide, so that the *volume* of his head stayed the same, but the shape changed, probably from all the things he crammed in there. By the time he died, on the first day of summer this year, his head was still longer than wide, but not by all that much.

There were a lot of things crammed in there: philatelic matters, German colonial history in Africa, mathematics, basketball trivia, ornithological amazements, Australian detective fiction, Polish science fiction, computer theory, Benedictine literature, a vast and amused memory of adventures with his wife and children, and a great deal of detail about their former dog, which was such an excellent dog that when she died the family never got another dog, not wishing to subject a second dog to inevitable adverse comparisons to the first dog, who could, among other feats, leap sixty inches from a standing start; one of my brother's enduring regrets, as regards this first dog, was that he and the children had not devoted as much time as they might have to teaching the dog to dunk a basketball, which would have been cool.

Though Kevin's head was enormous, his ego was not, and one of the interesting and admirable aspects of his character was that when you asked him a question about anything whatsoever you promptly received either an erudite answer or a terse admission of ignorance, which is not the usual dichotomy of response when you ask someone a question. Often when you ask someone a question, he or she hazards a response that quite often has nothing whatsoever to do with the matter at hand and everything to do with the respondent's political or religious mania, or the weather, or too much whiskey in the breakfast coffee. My brother Kevin, however, had the lovely habit of bluntly admitting that he hadn't the slightest idea as to the answers for a lot of questions, although he also had the unnerving habit of immediately finding out the answers and sending you a brief note in his tight scrawl a day or two later. It is amazing to me that a man with such a large head would have such small precise handwriting, but this was indeed the case.

Until very near the end of his life, his head was covered with a mat and jumble and sprawl of hair as thick in his sixties as it had been when he was six, which is also not always the case with men, although it is the case, apparently, with our family; our dad has said of our clan that we die young but never lose our hair, which is an awkward calculus, I feel, and which was true and untrue in Kevin's case, as he did die young but did lose his hair, although he maintained that *his* loss of hair didn't count, as it was caused by outside influences, as he said, rather than by the tide of time, which is an excellent point.

I remember his head looming over me as a child, mostly gently, although he did have a laser stare and a stern mask and a gruff tone that he used more as a fence than as a weapon, I suspect, although certainly many students over his career as a teacher quailed under his withering glare. And in recent years, as in the way of brothers growing older we grew to be the same age, and grew closer as friends, and grew closer as colleagues in wonder and laughter, I began to think that what had been stern and gruff and intimidating in him was perhaps a disguise for shy. He was a tall scrawny pencil of a guy in his opening chapters, the first living child of parents who had already lost a son, and the price of his intellectual brilliance, perhaps, was tension and tumult in other arenas; as a teenager he both joined and quit a navy at war, at enormous cost to courage and conscience. And he was that sort of man who warms as he ages, and year by year lowers another wall, fills in another moat, lays aside another lance, so that by the end he was publicly as gentle and funny and generous and open as he had always been inside his castle, in the years when he was a lonely king known only to a few.

A year before he died, I went for a walk with him, across the campus of the university he loved, the university he had graced as professor and counselor for ten years. By then he tottered a little, his castle frail and the dense thicket of his hair utterly gone; but every fifty steps, I tell you, a man or a woman or a lanky child would stop him, and hold his hand, or embrace him gently, and tell him how much they loved and admired and missed him and wished him well. He grinned, and didn't say much, but I walked behind him smiling that so many there knew him so well, knew him like I finally knew him, saw the wonder and laughter in his epic head. Walking behind him that day was like walking through the ruins of a castle that had once been frightening but was now just rubble from which something lovely had been freed.

his last game

We were supposed to be driving to the pharmacy for his prescriptions, but he said just drive around for a while, my prescriptions aren't going anywhere without me, so we just drove around. We drove around the edges of the college where he had worked and we saw a blue heron in a field of stubble, which is not something you see every day, and we stopped for a while to see if the heron was fishing for mice or snakes, on which we bet a dollar, me taking mice and him taking snakes, but the heron glared at us and refused to work under scrutiny, so we drove on.

We drove through the arboretum, checking on the groves of ash and oak and willow trees, which were still where they were last time we looked, and then we checked on the wood duck boxes in the pond, which still seemed sturdy and did not feature ravenous weasels that we noticed, and then we saw a kestrel hanging in the crisp air like a tiny helicopter, but as soon as we bet mouse or snake the kestrel vanished, probably for religious reasons, said my brother, probably a *lot* of kestrels are adamant that gambling is immoral, but we are just *not* as informed as we should be, in the end, about kestrels.

We drove further and I asked him why we were driving this direction, and he said I am looking for something that when I see it you will know what I am looking for, which made me grin, because he knew and I knew that I would indeed know, because we have been brothers for fifty years, and brothers have many languages, some of which are physical, like broken noses and fingers and teeth and punching each other when you want to say I love you but don't know how to say that right, and some of them are laughter, and some of them are roaring and spitting, and some of them are weeping in the bathroom, and some of them we don't have words for yet.

By now it was almost evening, and just as I turned on the car's running lights I saw what it was he was looking for, which was a basketball game in a park. I laughed and he laughed and we pulled over. There were six guys on the court, and to their credit they were playing full court. Five of the guys looked to be in their twenties and they were fit and muscled and one of them wore a porkpie hat. The sixth guy was much older but he was that kind of older ballplayer who is comfortable with his age and he knew where to be and what not to try.

We watched for a while and didn't say anything, but both of us noticed that one of the young guys was not as good as he thought he was, and one was better than he knew he was, and one was flashy but essentially useless, and the guy with the porkpie hat was a worker, setting picks, boxing out, whipping outlet passes, banging the boards not only on defense but on offense, which is much harder. The fifth young guy was one of those guys who ran up and down yelling and waving for the ball, which he never got. This guy was supposed to be covering the older guy but he didn't bother, and the older guy gently made him pay for his inattention, scoring occasionally on backdoor cuts and shots from the corners on which he was so alone he could have opened a circus and sold tickets, as my brother said.

The older man grew visibly weary as we watched, and my brother said he's got one last basket in him, and I said I bet a dollar it's a shot from the corner, and my brother said no, he doesn't even have the gas for that, he'll snake the kid somehow, you watch, and just then the older man, who was bent over holding the hems of his shorts like he was exhausted, suddenly cut to the basket, caught a bounce pass, and scored, and the game ended, maybe because the park lights didn't go on even though the street lights did.

On the way home, my brother and I passed the heron in the field of stubble again, and the heron stopped work again and glared at us until we turned the corner.

That is one *withering* glare, said my brother. That's a ballplayer glare if ever I saw one. That's the glare a guy gives another guy when the guy you were supposed to be covering scores on a backdoor cut and you thought your guy was ancient and near death but it turns out he snaked you good and you are an idiot. *I* know that glare. You owe me a dollar. We better go get my prescriptions. They are not going to do any good but we better get them anyway so they don't go to waste. One less thing for my family to do afterward. That game was good but the heron was even better. We already paid for the prescriptions so we might as well get them. They'll just get thrown out if we don't pick them up. That was a good last game, though. I'll remember the old guy, sure, but the kid with the hat banging the boards, that was cool. You hardly ever see a guy with a porkpie hat hammering the boards. There's so much to love. All the little things. Remember shooting baskets at night and the only way you could tell if the shot went in was the sound of the net? Remember the time we cut the fingertips off our gloves so we could shoot on icy days and dad was so angry he lost his voice and he was supposed to give a speech and had to gargle and mom laughed so hard we thought she was going to pee? Remember that? I remember that. What happens to what I remember? You remember it for me, okay? You remember the way that heron glared at us like he would kick our ass except he was working. And you remember that old man snaking that kid. *Stupid kid*, you could say, but that's the obvious thing. The *beautiful* thing is the little thing that the old guy knew full well he wasn't going to cut around picks and drift out into the corner again, that would burn his last gallon of gas, not to mention he would have to hoist up a shot from way out there, so he snakes the kid beautiful, he knows the kid thinks he's old, and the guy with the hat sees him cut, and gets him the ball on a dime, that's a beautiful thing because it's little, and we saw it and we knew what it meant. You remember that for me. You owe me a dollar.

the country of
who he used
to be

My late brother Kevin was once a tall skinny student at the University of Notre Dame du Lac, where he lived in an old residence hall on the south side of campus, between the cemetery and that university's signature golden dome. As a freshman he lived on the first floor, where most freshmen are consigned, but for the rest of his undergraduate career he lived in 327, at the top of the stairs, and it is this room, or set of rooms, that I wish to muse about this morning.

A sensible and informative essay would at this point remark on some architectural details of the three tiny rooms in which my brother and his three roommates lived, or would talk learnedly about the rooms' all-important proximity to the lone set of shower stalls on the floor, or note the view from the mullioned windows, or relate some of the entertaining and headlong adventures of the lanky children who lived there, or even go back today and chat with the lanky children who live there now. But I grope after something else about those rooms, about my brother's life in those rooms, about the seven hundred days and nights that he lived there, some fifty feet in the air above the sandy soil of northern Indiana.

The silent dawns, when he awoke in the top bunk, above a snoring roommate, and for a moment was back in his childhood bed, in the dapple of tall sweetgum trees outside his window, his mother's silvery laugh in the kitchen as faint as yesterday's hymn; the long winter nights, as he sat at his ancient desk, staring at the runes cut by a dozen previous denizens; the thump of basketballs and ricochet of footballs in the hallway, and the deep barking laughs of the burly neighbors who hammer and fling them; the autumnal smell of sawn wood as students edit their rooms, and the vernal scent of mothers in the hall, reclaiming their sons for the summer; the stammer of greetings to a friend's girlfriend, the cheerful roars at a friend's kid brother visiting in awe; the shouldery tumult and reek and jest of roommates, and the snarl of shoes and jackets by the door; the annual drawing of straws or cutting of cards for who gets which room; the wry notes left for each other, the casual generosity, the thicket of toothbrushes, the dank of towels and socks, the scrawl of numbers and names written on the yellow wall by the phone against all rules and regulations; and the way those names and numbers will be painted out, at the last moment, with paint of a wholly different color than the paint originally applied by the university when Indiana was young and dinosaurs strolled the earth.

He was nineteen when he walked into those rooms for the first time and twenty-one when he walked out, and I do not think he ever returned to them, though he returned to campus often, ostensibly for football games but more to visit the country of who he used to be; the residents of a campus change annually but the residence does not, and each long child who lives there adds infinitesimally to a story that can never be told in words. We thrash after ways to say what we know to be true, that the breath and laughter and tears and furies and despairs and thrills

the christmas letter

Greetings and salutations! A quick look at the year past in our family: The Woman of the House started a ska band, had a fistfight with a shopping cart, lost her right eye but then found it again under the couch cushions, and was the object of a terrific crush from one of the two very well-dressed boys who came to the door one day on behalf of the Church of the Risen Lord of the Swamps of Jesus. One boy started into a reasoned discussion of spirituality and community as the twin foundational pillars of the Church of the Risen Lord of the Swamps of Jesus and the other one just gaped and blubbered until he, this second boy, finally blurted out that she, the Woman of the House, was the very personification of his lifelong dreams of feminine allure, and if she could see her way clear to opening her heart to more than one husband, he, the second boy, could and would adjust his career plan with the Church of the Risen etcetera to include purchasing a ranch in Utah where perhaps societal norms were more open to committed love in other forms than the usual straitjacket of monogamous marriage. The Woman of the House declined but was deeply flattered and made a small contribution to the Church of the Risen etcetera, fine people, as she said later, tall, with excellent teeth. Dental hygiene is *very important*, as she says often, poring over a map of Utah.

Son One did have that unfortunate adventure with a weasel and a pumpkin but we report happily that son and weasel have both recovered, although the pumpkin was lost—a sentence that may never have been written before. Son One also enrolled at laundromat school this fall and has been studying diligently, words that never previously applied to him, but when a young person finds that one powerful driving interest in life, after an adolescence devoted to sneering, Victoria's Secret underwear catalogues, and expensive software, all you can do is be happy for him, and save your quarters in a pickle jar, isn't that so?

Son Two started out the year on a bodybuilding kick but working only on his left arm for some reason, and after he toppled over at the turkey rodeo in McMinnville and had to be hauled home on a boat trailer, he made some life adjustments, and we won't have to build that extra room on the west side of the house, after all! It's such a delight to see your kids come to grips with challenges in life, and bull their way through, whimpering gently and asking for money as if you are made of money, the very idea, do they not have the slightest iota of sense about money? They do not.

Our Lovely Daughter concluded her relationship with Biff, who mournfully then shaved off his mohawk, and we report that we are happy not to have to write or type or say the word Biff anymore, it just isn't a name that a sane mother would inflict on a child, all those consonants at the end comprising, essentially, a lip raspberry, ffffffffff, and the name as a whole seeming like something you would name a bison, or a pit bull, or the hero of a penny dreadful novel from the early 1920s. But we are getting distracted here with Biff, and will move along in this letter, but not before once again seizing the chance to excoriate the parents who stared at their new miraculous child, and, probably while drinking heavily or snorting pepper, named it Biff. The whole thing makes you revisit the notion that perhaps we should be required to obtain a license to parent, or at least there should be some basic rules for naming a child, like no more than four syllables, and no capital letters in the middle of the name suddenly for no reason, like LaMaQuisHa, and no naming a child for rainbows or seasons of the year or planets. Also you are not allowed to make up silly words, or name your child something without any vowels, or anything that ends with the letter i, or anything with a space in the middle of it. Nor can you name two or more children with the same name, which is just bad form no matter how many heavyweight boxing titles you have earned, and you may not name children for appliances or insects. You *may* name children for obscure angels and testy minor characters in whatever holy book you keep by the fire, but you must use a capital letter to begin. The rest of the year was lovely and we wish you and yours the best.

the necessary
spark

In the weeks before my grandmother died, she grew smaller and smaller until by the time she died she was the size of a bird. Her hair was white and she lay in a white bed in a white room. The building she was in was also white and there were nuns and nurses in white who sailed silently through the white hallways. It seems to me that no one ever spoke during that time. My grandmother's voice had departed this world before she did, and she was all eyes and bones and she and my mother stared at each other and no one said anything and I played in the corner of the room with sticks and feathers. Sometimes my mother let me go out on the grounds of the building and I would wander around amid the thin trees and dry brittle grass looking for sticks and feathers. It seemed to me that my grandmother was mostly sticks now. Her eyes were huge and she could see you no matter where you were in the room. Sometimes when I wandered outside I thought she could see me through the walls.

The windows in her room had white curtains. She was dying in the summer so the curtains fluttered and floated in and out of the windows all the times my mother and I were there. No one ever closed the windows day or night that I remember and I wondered why birds did not fly in and sit companionably on the edge of the bed staring at her silently like my mother did. My mother was made of eyes and bones also.

My father said my grandmother would never die because you have to acquiesce to death and she would not acquiesce to Jesus Blessed Christ Himself if Jesus came into her room and asked her politely. Jesus wore white after He died and came back to life and walked out of the tomb in which no one had been laid. Mary Magdalene said so and she was an Eyewitness as my father said. When he said those words you could hear the Capital Letter. My father said the Gospels would be much improved had someone deposed Mary Magdalene properly in the first few days after the Incident. My father said the women in my mother's family had wills so adamant and granitic that you could start a fire by using flint against their wills to get the necessary spark.

My mother said that the spark of life was slowly ebbing in my grandmother and that we would be derelict in our duty if we did not go daily to witness and escort it from this troubled vale. Every time we went, her eyes were bigger and her body was smaller and everything was whiter. The building was near the sea so that when you went out through the brittle grass and into the huddle of the trees looking for sticks and feathers you could smell salt and mist. My father said death is like the sea because people are swallowed quietly and are never seen again and there is no mark of their passage other than what you remember. I remember wanting to get as far away from my grandmother's enormous eyes as possible, and walking out of her room as soon as my mother nodded permission, and running out into the huddle of the trees, and sitting there in the shadows, playing with sticks and feathers. I cannot remember that I ever sat by the edge of her bed, or took her fragile hands in mine, or bent to kiss her enormous frightened eyes, or did anything except run away as soon as possible into the huddle of the trees.

When Jesus Blessed Christ died, everyone ran into the huddle of the trees except Mary Magdalene. My father said Mary Magdalene was a remarkable woman with a granitic will and a love bigger than the ocean and she ought to be acclaimed more than all the poor muddled apostles put together. After my grandmother died my father said everyone is so sad but we should be thrilled that she is now reunited with her clanswoman Mary Magdalene, and probably all the flinty women in history live in the same building in heaven where they can start cooking fires if necessary by using their granitic wills. Probably that building is so brilliantly white, said my father, that it can be seen even here on earth, if you look for it closely. Probably that is the star that sailors look for when the sea is near to swallowing them and they have one last appeal to make. Of course they would appeal to Mary Magdalene. Wouldn't you? Everyone else runs into the trees, but she would run right toward you in your hour of need and be there at the edge of the bed smiling when you awake.

the thorny
grace of it

The kids are surly and rude and vulgar and selfish and their feet smell so awful your eyes burn if you are trapped in a confined space with their empty sneakers or their unshod feet or both of those horrors at once, which happens. Your spouse can be testy and snappish and unfair and inconsistent and obsessed with finances and so liable to mood swings you have more than once considered erecting a barometer in the kitchen. The house is a shabby ragged moldy ancient peeling moist mess with so many tiny holes and apertures that slugs have their annual convention in the basement, with little tiny name badges and glossy registration packets and everything. The dog has barfed in every room in the house. The house is mortgaged until the day Jesus Blessed Christ returns in His Radiant Glory to resolve all mortgage payments and carry us home to His house. The yard is a dense chaotic jungle in which blackberry vines thicker than your leg have evolved to pick and choose which birds they will snack upon before eating the neighborhood cats for dinner. The street is a dangerous racing alley for supercilious young men with tattoos and muscle cars and beer bottles and bad attitudes. The neighbor across the way is a witch from the eighth dimension who has many times called the cops because children set toes on her pristine lawn. The rain it does not cease nor does it falter.

Your back has hurt since Reagan was president. Your daughter put a dent in the car so deep you can see China if the light is right. Not even the blessed toaster works properly. Your toothbrush smells like it was used to clean the parakeet's cage. Half the windows in the house do not open because they were painted shut right after the Revolutionary War and the other half have various cracks that look suspiciously as if they were caused by footballs and wiffleballs thrown by children who adamantly deny ever once in their whole lives picking up footballs and wiffleballs, the liars. There are plants more than twelve inches high growing in the gutters. There is a cedar branch bigger than Utah looming ominously over the porch. There are liars and charlatans in Congress. The oceans are fouled. There are millions of children in my country who will not eat tonight. There have been thousands of children raped in my beloved church. Many men and women I have loved with all my heart have withered and shivered and died. I have three brothers I will not meet in this lifetime and one I will meet again only when Jesus Blessed Christ brings me home to His house, wherein lives my brother who just died. My wife and I lost a child when he or she was smaller than my hand yet she or he was our child, a being unlike any other that ever was or will be, and I will not meet her or him until Jesus Blessed Christ leads me to her or him by the hand and we embrace, weeping. There is so much pain and loss and suffering and fear and helplessness and greed and violence that sometimes I lay abed and feel naught but a great despair, and cannot see how to go on.

But then I arise, because I know there are laughter and compassion, and creativity and wonder, and kindness and generosity beyond measure, and I know we are the tools and means by which light pierces the darkness. I know, as well and truly and deeply as I know anything at all, that the thorny grace of it is the shape and nature of its holiness. If there was no darkness there would be nothing for us to light. We are the light. So it is that I arise from the sagging old bed, and shuffle creakily into the glorious chaos of the kitchen, of my tumultuous family, of the bruised and bloody world, and get to work, grinning. I don't know Who set all this pain and glory in motion, but I bow in thanks for the sweet puzzle of it all. Amen.

There Are Many Ways to Pray

mr. kim

Mr. Kim is abrupt. He is brief. He is short. He is terse. He is direct. He does not beat around the bush. He brooks no nonsense. He is from elsewhere. He does not say from where. He does not like that question. He answers *elsewhere* when you ask that question. He may or may not be married and have kids. He does not answer that question either and generally then asks you if you are married and have kids and when you say stammeringly yes he says, See? Unnerving question, isn't it? Don't like people asking questions about your private life, do you? Me neither.

Yet Mr. Kim is kind. He is generous. He gives away loaves of bread without fanfare. He gives away cookies to children if they ask politely and say thank you. He once gave me a pound of butter. He once gave a man a sack of sugar so heavy that the man staggered when he carried it out the door of the bakery. He posts the athletic schedules of all local school sports teams in his windows. He pins up posters about lost dogs. He once pinned up a poster about a lost parrot even though he considered the chances of finding the bird slim to none. He does not pin up posters about lost cats because as he says privately, who cares?

But Mr. Kim is gruff. Mr. Kim is stern. Mr. Kim once threatened a prospective thief with a baker's peel, which is the large tool that you use to slide bread in and out of the oven. A peel has a wooden handle and a steel head bigger than an axe, and when Mr. Kim brandished it at the thief the boy ran out of the shop so fast he cracked his head a glancing blow against the door, which must have hurt like the devil but who cares? says Mr. Kim.

Yet Mr. Kim refused to press charges when the police actually caught the thief two blocks away, because as he said the boy did not actually steal anything, and so what exactly could he complain about? Nor did he fire the ancient janitor who came with the shop when Mr. Kim bought the shop, twenty years ago, even though it was soon apparent that the janitor did not actually janitate, as Mr. Kim said, but rather slept in the corner behind the stove after making a show of washing the mound of pots and pans inherent in a busy bakery. Mr. Kim did the janitating himself, I discovered, until the janitor grew so stiff and ill that he had to become a ward of the city, at which point Mr. Kim hired a boy who may or may not be his nephew or grandson; I have not had the courage to ask.

But Mr. Kim shouts in public meetings about zoning and redevelopment. He insults and excoriates members of the city council and tax commission. He gesticulates and offers vulgar remarks about people who obstruct the alley next to his shop in such a manner as to make deliveries impossible. He refuses to speak to the polite tiny women who run the barbershop next door because someplace in the past they did not join him in a petition the theme of which is now totally lost to history but not to Mr. Kim's long memory.

Yet Mr. Kim many times dug the snow away from the curb and pavement in front of their barbershop so that their customers could park and walk to their door. He filled their shop with twelve small candle-lit cakes one evening when one of their mothers died. After a terrific thunderstorm knocked out power on the whole block for three days and their fuse-box fried itself to death, he quietly paid for their fusebox to be repaired at the same time that his box was repaired.

But when one of the two women then came into the bakery to thank him for this kindness he denied that he had paid for the box, and was gruff and stern and terse, and said if you are not here to buy anything then you are obstructing customers, thank you, good-bye, and he gesticulated rudely when she stormed out of the store.

Why do you *do* that? I asked him, that time, moved by some impulse to ask him a personal question, even after many times learning that my questions were not welcome.

Do what? he said. What are you talking about? Are you here to buy something or ask questions? This is not the newspaper office or the library asking desk. If you are not here to buy something then you are obstructing customers, thank you, good-bye.

Yet when I bit my tongue to halt the snappish remark I would otherwise have made, and bought a loaf of his superb garlic bread, and cradled the redolent crinkling bag in my arms like an infant, and drove home with that exquisite scent filling the car like a song, and opened the bag with a flourish to show my family the glorious addition to dinner, out fell three cookies, one for each of our children, beautifully wrapped in brown paper so thin that when you held it up to the light you could see right through it, impenetrable as it seemed to be.

boots

Recently I met a quiet young woman who didn't say much but what she said was wry and pithy and direct, and after a while I asked if I could take notes as she talked, and she said okay, and this is most of what she said: My name is Jacqueline. You can call me Jackie. Until recently you could call me

Lieutenant. I am now retired from the service. I will be twenty-seven years old on Sunday, at fourteen hundred hours. I have a dog named Gus. I live near the beach. I was a hematology nurse. I am in good health, considering. I drink tea. I learned to love tea in Kirkuk. Some days we had tea ten times a day. We found a samovar and learned how to use it. There was a man among us who could play that thing like a guitar. It got so we couldn't drink anything other than the tea he summoned from the samovar. It was the most remarkable tea. He vanished one day when his truck was hit by the bandits. Another man took his place. He vanished too. I took his place. After a while I forgot everyone's names. For a while I called people by their numbers, but after a while I didn't call them anything. That's when I knew I had war sickness big time. I never got hit by fire but pretty much everyone I knew did. For a while there I thought it was me, that as soon as I said hello to someone or shook hands or learned their names they were doomed, so I stopped touching people and learning names.

You would think wigging out in the middle of the war would be bad but it's just normal. No one talks about what happens to the people nothing happens to, but something happens to them, and no one talks about it. Probably because we don't have any words for what happens. The fact is, wars kill words, but no one talks about that. Wars kill everything except more wars. Wars never end, they just hibernate and mutate and come back stronger somewhere else. Wars are the zombies of history. Some of what wars kill off you see getting killed off, like kids and towns and schools and Saturdays. But some of it you don't, like the birds. The birds don't nest in wars, you know, so pretty soon there are no birds, and then where are you, without the birds? What kind of world is that, with no birds in it? You notice things getting killed off little by little and then after a while you stop noticing things altogether. You don't even notice yourself. You just get by. By the end all I cared about was my shoes. You want really good shoes in a war. Trust me on this one. I had the best boots you could ever imagine, and I kept those suckers clean and oiled and ready for anything. When I got out of the war I kept wearing those boots for the longest time. I wore them with pajamas and with the bathrobe and with shorts in summer. It's only the last few weeks I go anywhere without those boots. Those are really good boots. When I am in those boots nothing can happen to me. Trust me on this one. I keep them on a special shelf at home, just in case. You want to know something real and true and honest and deep about wars? I'll tell you. Boots. Good boots are the secret. Really good boots.

a cricket match on bougainville, 1943

One time when I was in Sydney, Australia, I got into a conversation with an elderly priest who had spent most of his working life on Bougainville Island. We sat out under the gum trees, watching parrots whir by, and he told me about halting an incipient battle there once, between rebels and government forces, and about a boy he had known who people in the village thought was a fish in human form, and about one time a song was sung from one end of the island to the other without ever stopping, people singing it in turn for weeks, and many other things, and then he got onto cricket, which was his favorite sport, and which he had played as a boy and young man, quitting the pitch only when he was forty, in a ceremony attended by most of the people he had worked with on the island; in the course of this event he had burned his cricket bat on the field, and marked everyone's forehead with a smudge of the ash.

We were all laughing, he said, but there was a sweet reverence to the moment which I do not forget. There are more sacramental moments than we know.

Talking about cricket on Bougainville sent him back to one particular cricket match which he had witnessed as a prisoner of the Japanese Imperial Army in early 1943. The Japanese had taken the island in 1942, he said, and he was imprisoned with many other residents, both islanders and Australians. It was not an especially harsh camp initially, certainly nothing like the camps in Burma and Thailand, and they were allowed to read and play cricket and conduct religious services. But then as the war turned against the Japanese, and the Allies took a corner of the island, things grew darker. There is a great deal to tell of that time when things grew harsh, he said, but I wanted to tell you about this one day, when we decided to play cricket. It was a Sunday, and we set up stumps in the morning, and dressed in the best clothes we had left, and made up teams and assigned positions. One captain was a minister, a remarkable man, and the other was a teacher. The camp guards looked angry but no one stopped us. I opened the bowling. There was something desperate about the game; I suppose that's what I wanted to tell you. It wasn't like in the films, where we were making a statement to the oppressor. It was more like we were starving for something. I'll never forget that game. Everyone played as hard as they possibly could. I don't have the words for what it was we were so desperate for, but you could feel it in every man and boy. I have tried to tell people about this game before and they say things like nostalgia or courage or memory or peace but those are not the right words, somehow. They don't get deep enough. It's like if we had not been able to play that game we would have sickened and died. I don't know quite what else to say. We played all day. We didn't break for tea or lunch because we were afraid the guards would make us stop. We finished finally at dusk when one fellow jumped for a ball in the air and nearly caught a fruit bat. There

buying a foot

Friend of mine went to buy a foot the other day. Left foot. He lost the original in a war, and he didn't replace it for a while, being distracted by other things, as he says, but eventually he did replace it, first with a bamboo foot, which was a *terrible* foot, and then with a rubber foot he made from a tire, which was actually a pretty good foot, he says, and then with a series of wooden feet, which were pretty much totally worthless, and finally with a series of plastic feet, which are *much* better than wood or rubber feet or maybe even the original foot, he says, although the fact is I hardly remember that one at all because we parted company so long ago.

But recently when he was coming down a ladder, he broke his current foot, a plastic one, though he didn't discover it was broken until he got home that night and took off his boot and half his foot fell off.

I tried to glue it back together but it was just no use, he says, so I went to the foot store.

The foot store was founded by a guy who lost his leg in a war and carved a new leg from barrel staves. At the foot store you can buy all kinds of feet. You can buy feet with or without toes. You can buy feet made from plastic or steel or wood, although most feet in the foot store are made from carbon fibers arranged in a stunning number of ways. You can buy feet with toe and heel springs. You can buy feet with adjustable heel heights. You can buy waterproof feet. You can buy feet designed for golfing and rock-climbing and swimming and skiing and sprinting and snorkeling and scubadiving and mallwalking and hiking and tennis, among many other things.

You can also buy ankles and knees and legs at the foot store, and there are foot stores, says my friend, where you can also buy hands and arms and elbows, but the foot store he likes focuses on feet and has by far the best selection of feet in the city.

Most of the feet you can buy don't look like feet at all. They look like the sort of modern sculptures you might see in a hip downtown gallery and when you wander in to see them more closely out of sheer curiosity you notice the little white card with the price, which makes you gasp, and the irony there, says my friend, is that a good foot these days is just as shockingly expensive as hip art, many thousands of dollars, but when you need a foot you need a foot, so you buy one.

One time I asked him if he had ever tried to run with one foot and he said yes, once, about two years after I lost my foot, I had to run across the border of Vietnam and Cambodia at night, carrying my crutch and keeping my eye on a guy with a red shirt running in front of me. I didn't run, exactly, I guess, says my friend. It was more like I was hopping really fast. I was really afraid of losing sight of that guy. Well, I didn't lose sight of him, and he and I made it across the border, but it turned out that the Khmer Rouge were killing everyone on that side of the border, so eventually I came back across the border, but that time I had a boat and didn't have to hop.

At the foot store my friend got the basic model, no frills, size nine, and he's pretty happy with it, especially given the poor left feet he's had over the years, of which the worst had to be that bamboo foot, he says, which was just awful, it lasted about three days, but that was my first try at making a foot, which is a lot harder than it looks. And then I made three wooden feet, one from *camxe* wood, which is red, and one from *go* wood, which is black, and one from *sen* wood, which is gray, but then I made that rubber foot, and that was one good foot. You wouldn't think you could make a foot out of a tire but you sure can. I should have kept that one to show my kids, but at the time I was distracted by other things and not in a position to think about having kids or marrying a wife or anything other than figuring out how to make a foot and get the hell out of where I was, which was absolutely no place to be.

meat

My friend Tommy Crotty, who was a terrific basketball player in New York and went on to play college ball and be a cheerful husband and excellent dad before the idiot who just died in Abbottabad murdered him and thousands of other children of all ages on September Eleventh, used to call every big guy he ever played with Meat.

Hey, Meat, he would say to the lumbering earnest centers he played with, and hey, Meat, he would say to his tree-trunk power forwards, and even his whippet high-strung small forwards were all lesser Meat to Tommy, except in cases like mine where a guy played forward because none of the bigger guys who could rebound could score if you locked them in the gym for a week, and none of the other guards would go into the lane without a helmet and a crowbar, and I could at least convert easy shots and grab uncontested rebounds. So I started at small forward with two Meats, and Tommy ran the point with a succession of wild reckless gunners at shooting guard, which was a misnamed position on any team Tommy ran unless he trusted you to take decent shots and hit half of them, in which case he would deliver you the ball as if on a silver platter handled gently by an unctuous butler on Sunday.

He was a most amazing point guard, was Tommy Crotty, his name often all one word in the mouths of the coaches and refs and parents and fans who came to watch him slide like a grinning knife through what seemed like every team in the greater New York metropolitan area: *tommycrotty*. You would even hear this in churches and bars and one time at the police station, where there was a misunderstanding about an automobile until the sergeant realized that we played with *tommycrotty*, as he said, the word reverential in his mouth like he was talking about one of the Lesser Apostles. It turned out one of his kids was a ballplayer and the kid's team had gone up against our team and, hey, total respect for you other guys, I mean no decredation, said the sergeant, but our guys totally had your number except for your kid at the point, that kid is a magician, I never seen a kid do things like that with a basketball, and he is not the most athletic kid I seen either, which was true—Tommy was never going to be six feet tall and he was what his mother called husky, which is another word for unsculpted.

One time I asked Tommy why he called all the big guys Meat, and he said it was just easier that way, that learning their names was pointless because they all responded to the same simple stimuli, and names were excessive in regard to big guys, who were not the brightest stars in the sky. They want the ball early, you know, said Tommy, I think to reassure themselves that they exist, so I get each meat a basket early, and then they're *happy*, man. They are not the brightest bulbs in the galaxy. Once they score they are good for long stretches. Meat has short memories. Later in the half I get them another couple buckets each just to be sure they're awake. Otherwise I want them working for me, you know? Not worrying about scoring. I'll take care of the score, but I need meat work done out there, and *you're* not going to do it, prancing around like a hairy ballerina. At least *you* don't yell for the ball, which is why I give it to you when you're open. Some guys actually *yell at me* for the ball, can you imagine? Now, meat would *never* yell for the ball, they are better behaved than that, but once in a while a meat will set up his tent in the hole and wave for the ball. I wave back, man. Can you imagine signaling *me* to give *you* the ball? You don't think *I* know where the ball should go? Jesus. I had a meat once who was waving for the ball and I waved back and his face lit up and he shouted *hey Tommy!* This is why I call them meat, man. We have had some good meat here—remember that meat with the ponytail, that guy worked his butt off and never said a word, and he got rewarded for it, didn't he? He got the ball regular. Sometimes I was so proud of him for working so hard I'd give him the ball every other time down. You never saw happier meat. And to his credit he never got all artsy and cocky neither. I think because the ball was probably a shiny new toy to him every time he saw it, you know. I mean, the guy was a *center*, you know, so you keep your standards reasonable, you know what I'm saying?

This was how Tommy talked to us in the gym and the playground, but when he was talking to the coaches and refs and parents and fans who called him *tommycrotty* he used his Altar Girl Voice, all polite and reasonable and thanking the Madonna for what small gifts he had been given and stuff like that. You could melt butter in the mouth that otherwise pretty much had only the words *meat* and *good game* in it. He didn't talk on the floor at all except after a game when he was one of the few guys I ever knew who made a point of shaking every guy's hand on both teams and saying *good game* and actually meaning it, which is rare—most guys don't mean it at all and they would totally give you the finger if people weren't watching.

Well, the reason I wanted to tell you about Tommy was more than the entertaining way he called all big guys meat; it's about the time I absolutely hammered a guy on a blind pick in a game, and Tommy said something afterward that I've thought about a lot since he was murdered by the idiot in Abbottabad. The guy I clocked in that game was hammering Tommy the whole game, because basically Tommy was killing his team and the rest of us weren't, and this guy, I think his name was Rocco, figured he would cut the head off the snake, you know? So he bashed Tommy every chance he got, setting mean picks, cracking Tommy's hands and arms while supposedly going for the ball, really dropping the hammer on Tommy twice on drives to the basket, one time accidentally on purpose whipping a pass right in Tommy's face like the ball slipped but it didn't, and finally we had enough, and me and the meat set up a blind back pick, which is an evil basketball way to exact vengeance on a guy, he comes flying around the meat pick, a pick he expects and has seen all game, and then runs smack into a second vicious pick which he did not expect, the second pick being me with an elbow aimed at his eye. Well, the guy went down in a heap, and there was a ruckus with coaches and dads yelling and stuff, but the ref had seen the way the guy was bashing Tommy, and he figured an eye for an eye, so that was that.

But that *wasn't* that, it turned out, because after the game Tommy read me the riot act and told me never to do that again, not on his floor, or I would never see the ball again except in the shiny windows of sports stores, and more things like that. He said he understood why we had done it and he appreciated the thought but there was a right way and a wrong way to play and he would be damned if anyone on his team played the wrong way. I asked what about Rocco hammering him, and he said screw him, a guy like that you just play harder and show him the error of his ways. I said that was stupid and guys like that were idiots and would never see the error of their ways and the best

the ballad of
jimmy ward

Allow me the temerity of paraphrasing the late tart-tongued Mother Teresa: there are no great stories, only small stories told with great attentiveness. So I tell you a war story that has nothing to do with arrogance or fear or cash, the usual reasons we foment war. It has to do with a really lovely left-handed jump shot, the parabolic poem at the heart of the greatest of sports, the one invented in rural America long ago—our own wild sweet quicksilver tumultuous graceful gracious idiosyncratic basketball.

It's about a boy I'll call Jimmy Ward. He was the shooting guard for a basketball team here in the wild West. Point guards came and went on that team, forwards shuffled in and out, centers lumbered and plodded and were replaced by other massive slabs of meat, but Jimmy was eternal, Jimmy played every minute, year after year, because he had the quickest, deadliest, loveliest jump shot anyone had ever seen, and even the most martinettish of coaches knew enough to leave him alone and let him happily terrorize defenses with his sharpshooting. He had divine range and could drill that shot from anywhere; he was cat-quick and could get his shot off against the grimmest of defenders; and he had exquisite judgment and timing—he never took a bad shot, was liable to stunning hot streaks, and had the killer instinct granted to a few great players who understand exactly when a crucial score utterly deflates an opponent.

College scholarship offers piled up on the dining room table of his house; Jimmy remembers his father grinning as he riffled through the pile, reading the names of the colleges aloud in wonder, colleges who would pay handsomely to have his son as a member, colleges who wheedled and pleaded, colleges with names of ancient heft and glow. But Jimmy declined the glories of collegiate sport; he wanted to be a United States Marine, one of the few and the proud. He joined the Marines one day after he graduated from high school. Soon he was in a war. Soon after that he lost his left hand. Soon after the war he did enter college, this time on an academic scholarship. Eventually he became a teacher, a profession he enjoys today, a few miles from where he was the star of the basketball team. He coaches, too—the very littlest kids, on the theory, as he says, that if he can get them to run and pass and savor the looping geometry of the game, they'll have good basketball genetics when their bodies begin to rise toward the patient stars.

He can't shoot jumpers anymore, of course, not having a left hand, and while I watched him coaching the other day, smiling at the way he barked happily at the swirling minnows in his care, I wondered where his jump shot went. Is it in the steaming soil far away where his hand is buried? Is it only in the memories of aging men? What else is lost when we go to war? What trillions of other small wondrous gifts vanish when hands fire rifles instead of basketballs? What ways to war with one another have we not even imagined yet, ways that will reduce us still further? Are we ever going to grow up as a species and figure out how to find the country beyond violence? Are we ever going to stop saying one thing about violence and doing another? Are we ever going to really live as if joy is glory and blood is a crime?

Jimmy says we should have sports tournaments to solve international disputes—hey, sports is stylized war anyway, he says, why not take it to the logical conclusion, and have an epic conclusive Israeli-Palestinian soccer match, or a chess match between India and Pakistan for final possession of Kashmir? And why not have sporting punishments for criminals, like a competition between Osama bin Laden and Radovan Karadzic to see who can clean the most toilets of the families whose children they murdered? I mean, says Jimmy, why not have some fun instead of the usual murder, you know? Because wars are just lots of murders, he says. No one ever admits that in public, except the guys who used to be in wars, guys who got murder all over their hands and can't ever get it off again.

I'll end here, with Jimmy smiling at us, a lot of nothing where his left hand used to be. A small story, one guy, one hand, one war. But, you know, where *did* his jump shot go? And why?

the eighth
man

Here's a story. A young monk tells it to me, and then he and I just sit there for a while, by the abbey pond, watching the trout rise, neither of us saying anything, because some stories are so layered and riveting that you have to wander through them again slowly in your mind after you hear them the first time, like you wander back along particularly intriguing paths and beaches and streets, you know what I mean?

I think you do.

We have choir practice every other night here, said the young monk, and it's almost always pretty serious, although sometimes, usually in summer, we get a little giddy. Probably the late light, I guess. Well, it's always the same guys, of course. Seven of us, six of whom can sing and the seventh is just the most wonderful man although he couldn't carry a tune if it was a feather and he had a third hand. We make the same jokes, stand in the same places, make the same little singing errors. I mean, it's a monastery, and you get into certain habits and customs, just because we are here all the time, with the same guys, doing the same thing, day after day, year after year. I'm not complaining—the consistency is a sort of prayer itself, of course, and after awhile you get the sense that ritual and routine can be curiously freeing, rather than stultifying. I think when you are young you are terrified of ritual because it seems like the bars of a prison, but when you are older you appreciate rituals as strong trees you can lean on, you know what I mean?

I think I do, I said.

Well, one night we were at practice, said the young monk, and it was like any other night, I guess, with moments when we were all hitting our stride and other moments when four guys were on their game and two were not, for various reasons, and we started working on a song which I knew better than the other guys, so I moved to the front to be the teacher, basically, and I noticed that there were seven guys singing, not including me. It took me a minute to process this, because it was so weird—it's not like we get drop-in visitors, you know, and none of the monks who *don't* come to practice suddenly *come* to practice, that doesn't happen. So it took me a minute to spot the new guy. He was dressed like us, in the robe, but I had never seen him before, that's for sure. He sure could sing, though. Kind of a rough baritone, like Lou Rawls if he smoked two packs a day. Or Johnny Hartman before he got warmed up, you know what I mean?

I do, I said.

Well, in the monastery, you don't call guys out. It's not done. For one thing we don't talk more than is absolutely necessary, and for another there's a sort of let-things-play-out ethic here, just relax and things will become clear soon enough, we have plenty of time, so I just let him sing. I don't think the other six guys even noticed the new guy. We were in a good groove and there's a real pleasure in a good stretch like that when you are singing in a group. So we just kept going. We sang the new song through probably ten times, and then it was about time to close up for the evening anyway, so we tried it one more time, and this last time I thought we nailed it, each guy's voice fit right. Just lovely. When we finished, we all laughed and I noticed the guy was gone, just like that.

Now, I don't know what to make of this, said the young monk, and the more I think about it, the more I think maybe there's nothing to be made of it. A guy appeared out of nowhere one night, joined us for choir practice, sang beautifully, and then he vanished. No one else noticed him. I can assure you he was there; I am not a nut. He wore a brown robe. He had kind of a grainy baritone. He wasn't tall or short. That's all I can tell you. I never saw him again. I told the abbot about him, and the abbot listened carefully and after I was done telling him the story, and after we sat silent for a while the abbot said boy, we could sure use a good baritone. That's all he's said about it so far. So there's a story for you. If you wanted to treat it like a mystery there would sure be a lot of interesting details, like the choir door was locked the whole time, and we don't have any guys who sing baritone, and the gate on the road to the abbey was also locked, and to make your way on foot through the woods to the abbey at night is an adventure and a half, not to mention there are bears and cougars in those woods, and the biggest owls I have ever seen, you wonder if the owls up there go around picking up sleeping deer or what at night. But if you didn't want to treat it as a mystery, you could just marvel at the fact that a guy with a rough baritone showed up one night, sang the same song eleven times with us, and then vanished. I think maybe we spend too much time trying to figure out what stories mean rather than just marveling at the stories, you know what I mean?

I do, I said.

There didn't seem to be anything for me to say, after such a story, so the young monk and I just sat there by the abbey pond for a while, watching the trout rise. These are enormous trout, by the way. A couple of times I thought I saw a trout the size of a couch, but that might have been a trick of the light. One time I did see a very large trout rise after a dragonfly, which seemed awfully ambitious to me, but who knows what when it comes to possible and impossible, you know what I mean?

do wa do wa diddy

Okay, *here's* a story for you this morning. A young man in a monastery tells it to me. He's a brother, seven years in, still essentially the new guy, although as he says there actually *are* newer guys, but basically in our monastery any guy under the age of ninety is a new guy, which gives you a sense of the long-term attitude here; I mean, our monastery is more than sixty years old, but our sister monasteries elsewhere in the world still consider us a ragged outpost in the wilderness of the New World. One great thing about us monks is that we have a good sense of scale; if the Merciful One chooses to appear again in human guise in twenty thousand years, there will certainly be a monk who will grumble that He sure was in a hurry. You have to laugh. Anyway, the story I want to tell you is about one night in choir practice when things got hilarious and sweetly crazy for a while. We still laugh about it and I think maybe the story will be told here for, well, twenty thousand years, until the Merciful One slips in the chapel door and joins us Himself. You think He's a tenor or a baritone?

So here's the context: we warm up for choir practice by stretching, bending at the waist, swinging our hips from side to side, waving our arms like we are doing the wave, jogging in place. It always knocks me out to see guys nearly ninety years old shaking out their muscles like they are on the sideline getting ready to enter a basketball game, you know? Then we do some vocal calisthenics, some yawning, some mouth-stretches, just rattling off strings of nonsense words and numbers to get our lips loose, and on this night one of the guys started us off with a run of syllables like *nu wah nu wah nu*, and that slid right into *do wa do wa*, and then one of the older guys riffed on it as *do wa do wa diddy*, and that set us off. He had been in the Army, this guy, and he said later that his mind still naturally falls into cadence if he's not paying attention, and *do wa diddy* has a parade cadence, I guess, because off we all went, singing one *do wa do wa* song after another, "The Lion Sleeps Tonight" by The Tokens, and "In the Still of the Night" by The Five Satins, and "Earth Angel" by The Penguins, and "Duke of Earl" by Gene Chandler, and "Maybe" by The Chantels, although that one was hard because none of us can quite get up to that highest range. By then we were all laughing too hard to sing well anyway, and we were *supposed* to be practicing Ascension and Pentecost hymns, after all, and it's not like we had all the time in the world to fool around, you would be surprised how clock-bound monastic life is, and don't forget that we are all up before four in the morning every day to chant the first of five offices for the day. So we all sort of collected ourselves and got back to work, but at the very end of practice, just as we were about to head off in the four holy directions, the guy who had been in the Army said quietly *one more, fellas?* So we sang "Tonight, Tonight" by The Mello Kings, which is a really lovely song anyway, but imagine how lovely it sounds when sung by a gaggle of Trappist guys of all ages in a wooden chapel in a fir forest on an evening in autumn, one of those crisp clear starry nights when you can hear owls and crickets for a mile. I have to say it was one of the most beautiful and holy musical moments I have ever experienced. Who would have thought that a song by

dawn and mary

Early one morning, several teachers and staffers at a grade school are in a meeting. The meeting goes for about five minutes when the teachers and the staffers hear a chilling sound in the hallway. *We heard pop pop pop*, said one of the staffers later.

Most of the teachers and the staffers dove under the table. That is the reasonable thing to do and that is what they were trained to do and that is what they did.

But two of the staffers jumped, or leapt, or lunged out of their chairs, and ran toward the bullets. *Jumped* or *leapt* or *lunged*—which word you use depends on which news account of that morning you read. But the words all point in the same direction: toward the bullets.

One of the staffers was the principal. Her name was Dawn. She had two daughters. Her husband had proposed to her five times before she said yes and finally she said yes, and they had been married for ten years. They had a cabin on a lake. She liked to get down on her knees with the youngest kids in her school.

The other staffer was named Mary. She had two daughters. She was a crazy football fan. She had been married for thirty years. They had a cabin on a lake. She loved to go to the theater. She was going to retire in one year. She liked to get down on her knees to work in her garden.

The principal told the teachers and the staffers to lock the door behind her and the other staffer and the teachers and the staffers did that. Then Dawn and Mary ran out into the hall.

You and I have been in that hallway. You and I spent years in that hallway. It's friendly and echoing and when someone opens the doors at the end of the hallway a wind comes and flutters through all the kids' paintings and posters on the tile walls. Some of the tiles are clay self-portraits by kindergarten kids. Their sculptures were baked in a kiln and glued to the walls and every year there are more portraits, and pretty soon every tile on these walls will have a kid's face, and won't that be cool?

They jumped, or leapt, or lunged, toward the bullets. Every fiber in their bodies, bodies descended from millions of years of bodies leaping away from danger, must have wanted to dive under the table. That's what you are supposed to do. That's what you are trained to do. That's how you live another day. But they leapt for the door, and the principal spun on her heel and said *lock the door after us*, and they ran right at the boy with the rifle.

The next time someone says the word *hero* to you, you say this: There once were two women. One was named Dawn and the other was named Mary. They both had two daughters. They both loved to kneel down to care for small holy beings. They leapt out of their chairs and they ran right at the boy with the rifle, and if we ever forget their names, if we ever forget the wind in that hallway, if we ever forget what they did, if we ever forget how there is something in us beyond sense and reason that snarls at death and runs roaring at it to defend children, if we ever forget that all children are our children, then we are fools who allowed memory to be murdered too, and what good are we then? *What good are we then?*

There once were two women. One was named Dawn and the other was named Mary. They are who we can be. Don't let them be murdered again.

the woman in
the vast blue
coat

One morning long ago when I was on the pre-dawn bus from Chicago's north side to the city center, a passenger died. She was in the second row from the back, on the east side, facing Lake Michigan. The bus driver did not know her name. No one knew that she had died until the bus sighed to a halt at our usual final stop at Randolph Street and everyone shuffled off except the woman in the back. She was wearing a vast blue coat.

It was my habit to leave the bus last, because I liked the driver and often stood for a moment chatting with him before walking to work, so I waited for him at the door of the bus as he went back to wake up the woman in the vast blue coat. He was a gentle man, the driver, and he reached down and gently touched the shoulder of the woman's blue coat and said quietly, ma'am? Nothing happened and he waited another ten seconds or so for her to wake up slowly. As he said later, he himself knew full well what it was like to wake up on the bus when you did not remember you had fallen asleep, and there is an adjustment period of a few seconds as you shift gears from the dream world to this world, and you should be allowed those few seconds to shift gears, *and I try to run a gentle bus, considering the hour.*

He bent down a little then and spoke softly into her ear, but again there was no response and now he bent down fully and looked at her face closely, and then he knelt down. The way he knelt down is what I want to tell you about. He was no young buck, this bus driver, and kneeling down was no unconscious easy act, you could almost hear his parts creaking, but he knelt down slowly on both knees, and took her left hand in his right hand, and put his left hand first against the right side of her face, cupping her face for a second as you would the face of someone you loved, and then he put his middle fingers on her carotid artery, on the right side of her neck, to feel her pulse. He left his fingers there on the right side of her neck for about ten seconds. I saw this from where I was still standing motionless by the door of the bus. Outside the morning was brightening noticeably by the second, as if someone was pouring sunlight into the city with a huge measuring cup.

I believe this lady is deceased, said the bus driver. If you would be so good as to find a policeman, Brian, and the way he said this, the quiet gentle sad firm calm gravity of his voice, stays with me. I don't think I will ever be able to forget the way he said those words. He had turned his face toward me, to address me clearly, to issue what was essentially a polite command from driver to passenger, but I noticed that his right hand still held her left hand as a father would hold his daughter's hand, and that his left hand was again cupping her face as you would cup the face of someone you loved. I suppose that's what I also wanted to tell you about—the way his hands held her the way your hands hold someone you love.

I opened the door of the bus and stepped out to find a policeman, then and probably still now in good supply on the streets of Chicago, and there was a young brisk policeman right there on the corner of Dearborn, and we ran back to the bus together. The young policeman leapt up the steps and bent down over the woman in the vast blue coat for a few seconds and then he pulled out his radio. I had climbed the steps and was standing by the driver's seat in case there was anything else for me to do, and as the policeman spoke tersely into his crackling radio, the driver, who was still on his knees, turned to me again and lifted his right hand to me in a gesture that still makes me weep when I think about it. I suppose he was saying thanks, and also telling me that things were under control and I could go, but there was something else in it for which I cannot find the right words—something about witness, and sadness, and prayer, and the way your hands hold someone you love. I still think about his right hand, and the way he held it up with such grace and sadness, the way that it was more than a message. Maybe this seems like a little thing, the way a man thirty years ago held up his hand to another man one morning on a bus in Chicago, but I don't think it is little at all. I suppose that's what I wanted to tell you about, how a little thing like this isn't little in the least.

The Rich
Soil of the
Past

putting in the
screens

You kids won't know what I am talking about, but a thousand years ago, when I was young, every house would change its storm windows for screen windows in May. The screen windows were down in the cellar and they had been there since October and there were spiders bigger than basketballs living on them. To get the screen windows away from the spiders you needed a smaller brother for bait. The trick was to offer him to the spiders just long enough for a third brother to grab the windows while you extracted your little brother at the last possible second as the spiders raged and gnashed their epic and shining teeth. How families without at least three brothers managed to change their storm windows for screen windows every year was a mystery to me. Our dad said that only Catholic and Mormon families were able to have screens in their windows in the summer and that the other faith traditions had to swelter in the relentless heat and this was their penance for having strayed from the path. He said if you looked closely at windows as you walked or drove slowly through neighborhoods in the summer, you could see who had strayed from the path and who had not, and you could rest assured that the houses with screen windows were Catholic because Mormons were confined to Utah for tax reasons.

Once the screen windows and the roaring little brother had been hauled up from the cellar and hosed off, either your dad or your snarling oldest brother had to get up on the ladder and remove the storm windows without breaking more than one. The ladder was in the garage and it had been there since October and there were birds and small mammals living in it. Your sister volunteered to remove the birds and animals tenderly because she was a devotee of Saint Francis and all animals loved her and many lived in her room which our mom did not like, especially in spawning season. Instead of handing the immensely heavy storm window to you carefully from the ladder, your snarling oldest brother would drop it at such an angle that if you did not catch it just right it would cut your head clean off as if it had been cut by a machete. Our dad said that if this happened he would be sure to retrieve your head from the neighbor's yard and mount it on the mantelpiece whether or not your mother approved, which she certainly would not, as the mantelpiece was reserved for clocks and Jesus.

Once the screen windows were successfully installed and the holes where the spiders had honed their epic and shining teeth were repaired with glue and dental floss, then the storm windows had to be hauled to the garage, carefully and with a great deal of shouting and advice. This was an area where your sister shone, and she shouted more advice than anyone could possibly use in a century about where to place your stupid feet and what to avoid for God's sake and how God in His infinite mercy had not parceled out brains in an even and equable fashion in our family. When she was finished shouting in her high shrill voice like a testy cricket you knew you were inside the garage. The trick to stacking the storm windows properly in the garage was to use small mammals as your base and stack the windows at a slight angle and then cover them with a thick blanket stolen from your sister. Finally the ladder was placed nearby but not too near: What we are looking for ladderwise is proximity but not intimacy, said our dad, who added that we should all, each of his many and tumultuous children, take particular note of his phraseology here, and apply it later when we achieved the dense and prickly thickets of muddled and confusing adolescence. At that point the windows had been successfully changed, and our task was concluded, and yet another family duty had been executed in utilitarian fashion, said our dad, for which we should thank the bountiful mercy of Jesus, and we were released once again into the neighborhood, as free as the birds living in our sister's room.

november

Here is my mother, making sandwiches. It is seven in the morning. She is forty years old. John Fitzgerald Kennedy is president. She makes four sandwiches, one for each of the older children; the baby does not yet eat sandwiches, although there will come a time, not too many years hence, when he will eat more sandwiches in an hour than you would *believe* a boy could eat unless you saw him do it with your own eyes, as his siblings did, some of us watching with exactly the same sort of awed fascination with which you watch a lion dismember a deer. You would not easily believe that a boy, however tall or burly, could eat as many sandwiches in an hour as there were apostles; but I, Brian, heard and saw this, and I tell you it is true.

In another version of this story my mother would be making eight sandwiches, but three of her children do not eat sandwiches, whereas they live elsewhere, perhaps among the glittering stars, or perhaps dissolved into the uncountable growing things in this world, or perhaps pillowed in the billows of heaven, where they chat amiably with the One, and make bets about how many sandwiches total their kid brother Tommy will eventually be able to eat in an hour, God abstaining from the bet because He already knows that amazing number, and has in His subtle way provided the means by which our parents can obtain the ingredients thereof, the mustard and cheese, the thin slice of bologna when times are flush.

When she is finished with the sandwiches for the four children who are not wearing diapers today she makes another sandwich for her husband to take to work, and she listens to the droning news on the old yellow radio on the shelf, and she listens for the mewling of the baby who will someday mill through an incredible number of sandwiches on his way to being a tall and muscled person, and then this morning she pauses, and leans both her lovely hands on the kitchen counter, and weeps suddenly and silently for her three lost children, the three who went on ahead, the three who opened their eyes so briefly in this world, and milled the sweet holy air of this world with their infinitesimal lungs, but then all too soon ceased breathing, and so their spirits vanished from what had been lively squirming vessels for those miraculous spirits, and where their spirits reside today no one can say, not even the mother in which they lived for a time, curled and thudding beneath her heart.

But she dries her tears, and harries the children for school, and kisses her husband's tall thin grin as he leaves for work, and plops the cheerful baby in his chair by the old yellow radio, and issues each schoolchild a sandwich and a clean handkerchief and a brief lecture about scholarship (for) and fisticuffs (against), and hectors the schoolchildren out the door and through the fields, and sets about her whirlwind day, seven hours of relentless labor during which we believe she never rested for a moment, not even snatching a cigarette break in the garden, there to ponder the sparrows, who do not sow neither do they reap, though they do blithely steal seeds from the garden, it turns out.

I came home late that day, as I recall, just before dark, having been engaged in the social ramble of our populous street, and I found my mother once again in the kitchen, by the old yellow radio, with both her lovely hands on the counter, and again she was weeping, and I did not know why, and I was seven years old, and I was frightened, so I stood there silently, hoping that my father or grandmother would happen by and make things right again. But then finally I heard what the radio was trying to tell me, that the President had been shot, and that he was dead, and that no matter what scandalous revelations have squirmed forth since that day, no matter what scholars have concluded about his tenure, no matter how many drugs were in his system and lies in his mouth, he was a boy who vanished, he was one of us, a brief light in the long dark, and where his spirit lives today no one can say. His mother wept, remembering the months when he was curled and thudding beneath her heart; and many other mothers wept for him also. Thus passed John Fitzgerald Kennedy, on whose spirit we ask the grace of He who knows even the amazing number of sandwiches that can be eaten in an hour by one child among the incalculable number of children who have been, and are yet to come; and so amen.

sister anne

There was another nun in my school, when I was a boy, on an island, long ago, who did none of the jobs the other nuns did; and she comes back to me this morning, her robes rustling as she passed through the burble of the schoolyard at lunchtime, the sea of us children curling gently away from her on each side like the waves from the bow of a slender ship.

It was thought that her name was Sister Anne, her name taken for the mother of the Madonna, but no one knew for sure, and her sisters did not speak of her, to us, anyway; perhaps they talked among themselves, in their rooms and at table at night, in their white wooden convent beyond the tall wooden fence.

Neither teacher nor administrator, nor nurse nor counselor, nor missionary nor inspector from the motherhouse; neither deputy from the mother superior nor agent of the cardinal in New York City, nor even visitor, shy and cowled, from some other lost cousin of the One True Faith like the Maronites and the Syriacs, the Coptics and the Malabars, the Melkites and Ruthenians—she was a mystery, though she passed through us every day at the same hour, a moment before noon Mass was said in the old church; never early and never late, never a glance astray from her destination, never a word for a child, even for those like me who sometimes stopped and stared, and wondered who she was and from whence she came.

161

Age? Ageless, in the way of nuns, who are young as new flowers or aged anywhere from thirty to seventy. Dress? The same as her sisters in the Order of Preachers, white and black, their huge rosaries swinging like burnished brown chains from their belts. Her face? Framed by coif and wimple, draped by veil, all hints of hair and ears hidden from the eyes of others. A simple silver ring on her left hand, as befits a bride of the Merciful One; the sturdy simple high black shoes of her time; a purposeful stride married to a casual grace, so that she neither hurried nor dawdled, ambled nor arrowed, but walked easy and intent to Mass, for reasons of her own.

As an altar boy I would occasionally serve the noon Mass, a sparse affair populated mostly by the very old and the ostentatiously pious, there for their second Eucharist of the day, the bag limit for miracles on your tongue in chapel; and from the altar I could see Sister Anne, always up in the balcony to the left, always under the stained-glass window of Stephen the Martyr, always alone; she would descend for the Eucharist and then stand in the shadows by a side door until the words *ite missa est*, the Mass is ended, go in peace, and we chanted *deo gratias*, thanks be to God, and she was gone, evanescing back through the now-empty schoolyard and behind the tall wooden fence and into the convent where no child ever went except into the warm and redolent kitchen where lived round and gentle Sister Cook, who made sandwiches for those of us who had forgotten or lost or been robbed of our lunches.

Of her stories and sorrows, loves and labors, despairs and ecstasies, name at birth and hour of death, I know nothing, and to poke into the annals of the Sisters of the Order of the Preachers of that time on that island would be only journalism; my purpose here is something else, something I cannot quite find words for, despite all these years of handling and shepherding words, and asking them to say more than they mean. I want to *see* Sister Anne again, for a passing moment, and have you see her too, as clear as we can, as the schoolchildren make room for her with quiet awe. She gave her life to the idea that there is a love greater and wilder and sweeter than anyone could ever measure. *She gave her life.* Have we ever thanked those women enough? Have we? No. But we can see this one, for an instant, and reach out to her, and say bless you, Sister, bless you and your sisters, bless you, bless you all.

the brilliant
floor

There was a girl named Linda in my first-grade class, at Saint
John Vianney School in New York. She was shy and tall. She sat
in front of me in the first row. We sat in alphabetical order, so
that Accopardo was first seat first row and Wyzkyski was fifth
row last seat. It was easiest that way for Sister Marie. She was
also shy and tall. She was calm and tender and firm and maybe
twenty years old. Most of us were six years old but four of us
were five. Linda and I were among the fives. The sixes looked
down on us as soon as they discovered we were five. They discovered this within the first week of school, and after that there were
the sixes and then there were the fives. Why that should matter
is a puzzle, but it did.

One day, after a particularly turbulent recess in the playground during which all four of the fives had suffered some
indignity from the sixes, we trooped back into our classroom.
In Sister Marie's class you were expected to carry the detritus
of your lunch back to your desk, so that she could be sure that
you had indeed taken sustenance; but this day Sister noticed that
Linda's lunchbox was empty. No sandwich wrapper, no cookie
crumbs, no apple core. Sister inquired; Linda sat mute. Sister
pressed, gently, leaning down to Linda at her tiny desk; Linda
covered her face with her hands and wept. Sister realized that

Linda had been robbed of her lunch by the sixes, and had not eaten at all, and had been humiliated by the theft, and was more humiliated now by public revelation, and Sister straightened up and stared at each of the sixes, her face unreadable, but just as she began to speak, Linda sobbed even harder, and a rill of urine trickled from the back of her seat and pooled on the floor between the first and second rows.

For a moment there was a ruckus as some children shouted and leapt away from the pool, but then Sister said Silence! Seats! very firmly indeed—not shouting, but so firmly that everyone sat down in silence—and then she appointed Meghan to lead Linda to the girls' room and then to the school nurse. Meghan held out her arm just like a gentleman does in old movies, and Linda took her arm and they stepped over the puddle and left the room. You could hear Linda sobbing all the way down the hall.

The best reason we have schools, I think, is to learn things for which we do not have words or equations. All teachers admit that their students will remember very little, if anything, of the curriculum they were taught; in the end what teachers really do is offer context, manners of approach, and the subtle suggestion that a cheerful humility before all problems of every sort is the only way toward useful grapple, let alone solution. What teachers really teach, it seems to me, is not a subject, but ways to be; a poor teacher teaches one way, and a fine teacher teaches many, some of which may be, to your amazement and relief, ways for you, the student, to open, to navigate, perhaps to soar.

Sister Marie was a fine teacher. We sat silently for a long moment, after Linda left, and then Sister sent a boy to the men's room and a girl to the girls' room to get all the paper towels they could carry. They came back with one million paper towels. Sister gave each one of the sixes a handful of towel and they mopped up the puddle, one by one, in alphabetical order, by rows. They did this silently. When they were finished, Sister handed each of the remaining fives a handful of towel also, and we also knelt and scrubbed the brilliant floor. No one said a word. The sixes then collected our paper towels and put them in the trash. A little while later Linda and Meghan came back and sat down and we started into arithmetic. I never forgot this lesson, and I would bet that no one there that day ever did either. I would bet the house on that.

sister cook

When I was a Catholic schoolboy, several hundred years ago, the custom of our teachers, each and every one a Sister of the Order of Preachers, was that if you forgot your lunch, or had it stolen under assault and occasionally battery, you were sent, curiously without ignominy, to the adjacent convent, where Sister Cook, a spherical woman with serious muscles, would make you a peanut butter and jam sandwich, or a peanut butter and honey sandwich, your choice; and you would eat your sandwich at the huge old wooden table in her kitchen, a table as big and gnarled as a ship, as she bustled about doing this and that, and she would offer you milk or water, your choice, and she never had a tart or testy word for you, but would even occasionally haul up a tall wooden stool to the table, and perch upon it, as golden dust and swirls of flour drifted through the redolent light, and ask you questions about your family, all of whom she knew, partly because your brothers and sister had sat at this same table, and eaten of the Sisters' bread and honey, and then been sent back through the tiny lush convent garden and through the vaulting wooden fence, emerging into the chaos of the schoolyard, where screaming children sprinted this way and that, some grabbing each other by the hair or necktie, until the bell rang, and we again fell into lines ordered by grade and teacher, and shuffled burbling back into the echoing hallways, therein to be educated.

Many a man has written elegiacally or bitterly of his education under the adamant will and firm hands of the Sisters, but not so many have sung the quiet corners where perhaps we were better educated than we were in our classrooms, with their rows of desks and pillars of chalk and Maps of the World. Perhaps I learned more about communion at that epic timbered table in that golden kitchen than I did in religion class. Perhaps I learned more about listening as prayer from Sister Cook than I did from any number of speakers on any number of subjects. Perhaps I soaked up something subtle and telling and substantive and holy about service and commitment and promise from Sister Cook, who did not teach a class, nor rule the religious education curriculum, nor conduct religious ritual and observance in public, but quietly served sandwiches to more small hungry shy children than anyone can count, in her golden redolent kitchen, with its table bigger than a boat.

Sometimes there would be two of us, or even three, sitting quietly at that table, mowing through our sandwiches, using two hands to hoist the heavy drinking glasses that the Sisters used; they must have had herculean wrists, the Sisters of the Order of Preachers, after years of such glasses lifted to such lips; and Sister would wait until all of us were done, and we would mumble our heartfelt gratitude, and bring our dishes to her spotless sink, and be shown the door; and never once that I remember did any child, including me, ever ask her about herself, her trials and travails, her delights and distractions, what music she loved, what stories, what extraordinary birds; we ran down the path toward the vaulting wooden fence, heedless; and only now do I stop and turn back and look her in the face and say thank you, Sister Cook, for your gentle and delicious gift, which was not the sandwich, savory as peanut butter and honey can be, but you.

mister ward

One evening, a long time ago, when the world and I were young and our Boy Scout Troop was just finishing up its monthly meeting, during which the various patrols competed in woodcraft and the pursuit of merit badges, and one patrol, the Red Foxes, had exhibited its research project into the culture and daily life of the aboriginal peoples who had once lived on our island but now were long gone leaving only the name of our hamlet, our troopmaster, Mister Ward, asked me to stay behind, as the other boys trundled home.

And when they were all gone, and the only other soul in the cavernous room was the assistant troopmaster snapping up chairs, Mister Ward and I sat on the edge of the ancient wooden stage, and he asked me gently if I really wanted to be a Boy Scout, and if I had any ambition whatsoever to rise to the next rank from the netherland where I had dwelt peacefully since entering the Scouts.

He asked if I was intimidated, perhaps, by the exploits of my older brother, who had been a remarkable Scout, or by my younger brother, already rising rapidly through the ranks, and if I had any inclination at all to eventually pay or at least make a gesture toward paying the dues I had owed since entering the order? And had I any inclination whatsoever to participate with any interest whatsoever in any activity whatsoever other than summer camp in the forests of the north, in which I had evinced great interest, despite total lack of woodcraft, said avid interest being perhaps, suggested Mister Ward gently, more a function of being assigned to a tent with my three best friends at the time, all excellent Scouts who tended to cover for me in any Scouting endeavor, than any, shall we say, significant personal interest in the ideals and practices that we have come to expect in this troop over the years, the very ideals at the heart of the Scouting movement itself as envisioned by its estimable founder Lord Robert Stephenson Smyth Baden-Powell?

I remember his gentle face, Mister Ward, a little worn with care and work—he ran the dairy—but open and patient, his spectacles just a hint awry, his crewcut like a lawn that had been meticulously mown weeks ago but a few patches were working up toward the light a bit faster than their compatriots, giving him a slightly uneven ceiling, and his worn but pressed uniform, complete with Scouting kerchief bound with a beautiful tooled leather holder called a woggle—funny the words you remember from previous lives, and funnier the extraordinary level of detail: I remember there was a black bear's face artfully burned into the woggle, its piercing eyes staring at me from Mister Ward's throat as he gently issued a speech that must have been awkward to contemplate and harder to deliver, for he was, it soon became clear, inviting me gently to retire gracefully and in good order from Scouting, inasmuch as I could not honestly claim an iota of ambition or genuine interest in any aspect of the idea, other than summer camp in the forests of the north as aforementioned, and even there, said Mister Ward gently, he had noticed that my tentmates tended to carry me surreptitiously in group endeavors, which he admired, collegiality and true friendship being, of course, root virtues of the Scouting movement, to which he had lent his own energies for years now, initially as patrol leader and then assistant troopmaster and now troopmaster, in which capacity he found himself obliged to occasionally have discussions like this one, and did I have anything particular I wished to say along these lines?

He must have been all of about forty then, Mister Ward, although to me he seemed craggy and ancient beyond measure, with gray wings in his cropped hair and fingers yellowed by his cigarettes, but I remember how gentle he was that night, almost rueful, almost a little sad—not, I think, because he was asking me to leave, or because I did not love what he loved, but because at heart it pained him to set a boy adrift. We did not know each other well, we had hardly spoken in my brief tenure in his troop, and while he knew what I did not want, he could not see what I did want; nor did I, then, which he also knew, and which worried him, I think, deep down.

Ever since that night, some forty years ago now, I have told this story with high glee, savoring the oddity of being the rare boy asked to leave the admirable Scouts for total lack of ambition, and thus of course actually celebrating myself, trumpeting my individuality, peering from the forests of comedy. But now, writing it all out this morning, it seems to be not about me at all, but about him, about the grace and pain of a good man. It was hard for him to say what he said, and all I heard was me; and it took me forty years to understand that he must have steeled himself to speak that night, and stayed late from his own family to try to help a boy he hardly knew, a boy he would never see again, a boy he could only hope would find a road that riveted him.

I did find that road, eventually, and have tried to walk it since, listening for stories of quiet grace, the accounting of which is my work; the celebrating, that is, of people like Mister Ward. There

40291

If huge things, like an education at the University of Notre Dame du Lac, which we collectively believe to be a different sort of creature than other educations for subtle and elusive but nonetheless substantive reasons, are composed of zillions of little things, not one of which is little and every one of which occurs under the sharp eye of the Coherent Mercy, then it matters somehow that our clean laundry came back from the laundry building wrapped in crackling brown paper and bound meticulously with string; and it matters that each boy (for only boys had their wash done by the university in those hoary days three decades ago) had a laundry number, five digits, printed on clean white cloth, and issued the summer before you enrolled, so that your mother, almost certainly your mother, in those hoary days three decades ago, stitched every scrap and bit of your few articles of clothing with your number.

And it matters somehow that this morning, when I open a Paleozoic drawer and discover a faded cloth ribbon nineteen inches long with a procession of my laundry numbers, everything everything everything floods back over me, and I laugh and weep at once: for the shy eager frightened boy I was that summer; for the hours I never knew or cared that my tiny fiery patient mom sewed those numbers to my shirts and jeans and socks and towels and one dark wool suit jacket suitable for Mass *because you will go to Mass every few days, won't you, son?*; for the cheerful vulgar gentle roommates who so often hoisted my bundle with theirs on their ways back to our hall, the greatest hall there ever was no others need apply; for the blessed paper and holy string, o the string the string, someone in the laundry carefully binding the bundles, each as big as a pillow, all day long, hundreds per day, each wrapping of the pile of clothes an act of love and reverence in the final analysis, each deft weaving of string a prayer of incalculable proportions, yes, for *we can do no great things, only small things with great love*, said that tiny sinew we call Mother Teresa.

And again and again some kind soul bound my battered jeans and tattered shirts with sturdy crinkling butcher paper, snapping the corners in with practiced sleight of hand, and whipped string into a tight crisscross so fast the package had no time to complain, and slid the bundle down the line, eventually to be picked up by a burly humming lad from Kentucky, or the slums of Philadelphia, or a fishing town near Seattle, and carted across campus as if it weighed an ounce, which on those careless young shoulders it did, once upon a time. In your room it would be torn open without a thought, a shirt grabbed because *we have exactly eighty seconds to get to Emil, man, let's go!*, the paper later a wadded weightless weapon fired at a razzing roommate, the string used for emergency shoelaces, and not a hint of a thought, not a shard, for the unknown holy being who washed and wrapped the clothes on your back, or she who stitched those numbers to your clothes, or he who bought the clothes, or she who got a second job to pay your tuition, or they who lay awake at night silently wondering if you were safe, and healthy, and happy, and going to Mass every few days, and wondering if they had given you enough of a launch pad, enough sweet tools to carry you forward into the kind of man you might be. Perhaps

somehow you became that man; and perhaps you open a Meso-
zoic drawer one morning, and find a faded cloth prayer with a
parade of your laundry numbers, and wonder if you ever could
say thank you enough, to everyone who ever blessed you in the
incalculable ways we are blessed, and you realize you cannot; but
you can try.

the stick

I have never been arrested (yet), but I *have* been asked politely to accompany a police officer to the local station to sort out what he called a misunderstanding, and it is that bright crystalline afternoon, on a beach, that I wish to recount here.

I had been strolling along the beach with two college friends, one of whom had never had a drop of drink in his life, and the other who had, that day, too many. He was in a cheerful mood, addressing raffish remarks to passersby, until one passerby was an officer of the law, who stopped us and inquired as to our collective sobriety. We sober gentlemen reported ourselves so, and we made gentle excuses for our companion, who stood swaying gently as we explained that he was not altogether what you would call sober, but we were escorting him safely back to a place of rest, and we were not driving, or armed, or contemplating any other flouting of the law other than intoxication on the beach, which, however, applied to only a third of us, all things considered.

The police officer, as I remember, was a youngish man, sturdy and tanned, and while he seemed slightly amused, he was not *very* amused, and his inclination to be unamused became evident when he asked our unsober friend what was in his pockets, and our friend replied, in a much clearer firmer voice than you would expect from an intoxicated young man replying to a question from a policeman,

Why don't you reach in there and find out, copper?

He said the word *copper* with a particular flourish, just like he was in a movie and he was a gangster making a terse remark about an officer of the law, and perhaps it was this little extra emphasis that tipped the cop from slightly amused to *come with me, boys* because *come with me, boys* is what he said, tersely, and this we did, dragging our friend.

The police station was only a block inland from the beach, and it looked more like a lifeguard shack than a regular police station, but inside there were other burly policemen, and a booking sergeant, and a forbidding drunk tank, and posters of wanted men on the walls, and the jangle of handcuffs on belts, and I saw, for the first time in my life, a nightstick, sitting on the booking counter in front of the grim sergeant.

Now, a nightstick doesn't *sound* fearsome—I think it's the word *stick* that dilutes the word, *stick* being a cousin of *twig*—but when you see one up close you have a lot of respect for the inherent and incipient violence of the thing. It is a weapon, sure enough, and I stared at it for a while, contemplating how a muscular policeman with his feet set could deliver a terrible cracking blow to a head or a shoulder or an arm flung across your face to protect your eyes and brains.

Well, the misunderstanding was cleared up fairly quickly, and stern admonitions were issued, and vows and promises sworn, and every time our unsober friend opened his mouth to make some witty remark he got an elbow sharp as a stick in the ribs, so much so that he said his ribs hurt for days afterward, and soon enough we had been bundled back onto the beach and were slogging through the sand with our friend, who began to sing. I believe he was singing the Beach Boys, but I am not quite sure now.

For years afterwards my sober friend and I told this story with glee, because there is a comic element to it, but curiously now what comes back to me first when I think of that brilliant crystalline afternoon is not the foolish remark, or the essential calm of the policeman, or the sadness of the drunk tank, or the Beach Boys, but that nightstick on the counter. We have hammered each other with sticks for a million years now, and even now that we have invented the most astounding and devious weaponry, we still lean on sticks and rocks when we lose our tempers and wish to bash out the brains of our cousins. All my life I have spoken against violence in some forms and loved it in others, and now that I near sixty I despair of ever rooting it out from my own heart; and every day, I tell you, every day, I wonder deep in my soul if we will ever evolve to the point where we have finally lost the urge altogether, and settle our arguments with chess, or laughter, or games of darts. When I was younger I was absolutely sure that there would come a day when to see a nightstick you would have to visit a museum; now that the night is ever so much closer for me, I am not so sure. Will you tell me, can you tell me, that this will come to pass? That however many of us are convinced, that is how much closer it is?

mister burns

At about ten in the morning on my first day as an assistant editor at *U.S. Catholic* magazine, then housed very nearly under the elevated train tracks in downtown Chicago, I was summoned to the august sanctum of the Executive Editor of the Magazine, one Robert E. Burns, known to one and all as Mister Burns. No one knew what the E. stood for although there was a great deal of headlong speculation. Mister Burns wore a lovely burnished silver-gray suit and had the roundest pleasantest ruddiest Irishest face you ever saw until he opened his mouth and said tersely There are several rules here that you ought to know about from your opening moments with us. We do not begin a sentence with the word hopefully. We do not use pointless words like ongoing. We discourage adverbs. We do not conclude pieces in the magazine with cosmic foolery like "it remains to be seen." It does *not* remain to be seen. We do not use such foolery as "on the other hand." There are no hands in this magazine. We do not edit quotes without that most useful of tools, the ellipsis. We do not respond to lunatic letters with sarcasm or ostensible wit even if they are from John Cardinal Lunatic. The most useful phrase I know is "you may be right." We respect authorities of every kind but we do not accept their pronouncements at face value and by the word authorities here yes I do mean Our Holy Mother Church. We do not use other languages in the magazine without a very good reason. Anything that can be said in

179

another language can be said better in American English. There is free coffee in the mail room but you are expected to be reasonable in its consumption. The use of pens, pencils, typewriters, fax machines, reams of paper, and books and periodicals from the library is not monitored by employees but you are expected to be reasonable in their consumption and return the books and periodicals. We will assume by the fact of your employment that you are aware of the history and traditions of Catholicism in America but this is not a historical magazine. We are interested in stories that have something to say about Catholic life in America. We are interested in Catholic life elsewhere in the world but not as interested as we are about Catholic life in America. We are interested in religious and spiritual matters of all sorts but a piece about Hindu life in Australia, for example, would have to be a hell of a fine piece to beat a piece about Catholic life in El Paso, Texas. We expect you to learn to at least grapple with photography, assignment letters, negotiating payment for authors, recruiting authors, discovering and sifting ideas, editing authors whether they like it or not, and contributing occasional pieces of every sort to the magazine yourself in time. However this is not a literary salon and you are not employed to become a writer on company time. You are employed to be an editor at a damned fine Catholic magazine in the United States. What editing actually entails you will have to find out for yourself. Inasmuch as I know and esteem your mother and father, I believe you have a genetic leg up on the task but I have been unpleasantly surprised by genetic collapse before and I am sure it will happen again. Let us hope that I am not speaking presciently about you. In the event that you do turn out to be a decent writer, which is all we can safely hope for on this God's earth, remember that we do not pay extra for contributions to the magazine, and that your contributions to other magazines, which we in general encourage, even for Jesuit magazines, should be composed and polished on your own time and in your own domicile. I believe that covers the general outlines of expectations and responsibilities as you begin with us. I will assume that you have no questions because you are eager to get to your desk and advance the interests of the magazine, an admirable urge. My best wishes on your work. Close the door gently when you leave. If you see an adverb out there, kill it. I think that covers everything.

the green
seethe of
the sea

We go to the shore as we sit by a fire: for some ancient solace, some peace older than culture; long before we could try to explain it in words, we stood on beaches and promontories and stared at the sea.

For the endless vista, yes, and for the ceaseless energy of the waves, yes, but for other reasons too, and those are subtle, and they say something of our deepest selves.

For isn't there some peace in the immensity of the ocean, some perspective? Our problems cannot be larger than the ocean. The ocean is patient. We can sit there for hours, huddled in a blanket, and after weeping there is a peace in the eternal ebb and flow of it. It never ends. It is a music. We are salt water ourselves, of course. We know that music. We heard it in the womb. We go back to it when we need to. We know it's there waiting. It doesn't ask questions or give advice or make pronouncements or ask you to summon courage and rebuild your life. There's a peace in that. It murmurs but it has no expectations for reply. There's a peace in that. It is neither a mountain, silent and epic, nor a lush forest, loud and dense. It is alive but not alive. There's a peace in that. It's so much bigger and older than any and all of us that it's frightening and alluring. It doesn't care about you, and there's a peace in that.

In summer we sit by it and pretend to read and after a while the words blur and the story fades and there's sun and sand and breeze and the thrum of surf and the piercing shouts of kids and gulls and you have forgotten what time it is. You have forgotten to even think what time it is. It is either late or not yet. In winter we walk along it and shiver in the whip of wind and your cheeks burn and your heart leaps and there's no one for miles and it's either time to go get warm or not yet.

We stare at the horizon like it was a language we don't speak yet. We stare at the shift of clouds and the leap of light and the green seethe of the sea. Even the biggest boats look fragile and the biggest ships seem tiny, in the end. There's an enormous tanker on the horizon and in the immensity it's smaller than a thimble. We are absorbed by shipwreck stories because we have a thousand times imagined sinking down into the silent abyss. We are terrified by the sea and we love it and we cannot do without it. Those who live far away from it yearn for it and those who live by it have never seen it the same way twice. Our houses fall into it and we rebuild our houses closer. We starve for it. We come around that one particular corner of the valley where the fingers of fog probe inland deepest and we lower our windows and breathe it in like a moist song and the wind roars in the car like the sound of the sea.

We make magazines to try to say some of the story. We make music set there and inspired there and trying to sound like the sea. We set movies and books there. We marry there and scatter our ashes there. We starve for it and do not have the words to articulate our hunger. So we write essays, here and there, to try to say something small and true about how we love and are terrified by and love the sea. We could not live without it. Each of us is a small sea with salt water swirling in us like a tide, and every drop of liquid in you passes through your heart. Is it any wonder we are always looking to the sea?

about the author

Brian Doyle is the editor of Portland Magazine at the University of Portland, in Oregon. He is the author of four essay collections, most recently *Leaping: Revelations & Epiphanies* (Loyola Press, 2003). He and his father Jim Doyle are the co-authors of *Two Voices*, which won the Christopher Award in 1996. Brian's own essays have appeared in *The American Scholar, The Atlantic Monthly*, and *Harper's*, among other periodicals, and in the *Best American Essays* anthologies of 1998, 1999, and 2003.

Continue the Conversation

If you enjoyed this book, then connect with Loyola
Press to continue the conversation, engage with other
readers, and find out about new and upcoming books
from your favorite spiritual writers.

Visit us at **LoyolaPress.com**
to create an account and
register for our newsletters.

Or scan the code on the left
with your smartphone.

Connect with us through:

 Facebook
facebook.com
/loyolapress

 Twitter
twitter.com
/loyolapress

 YouTube
youtube.com
/loyolapress

Also by Brian Doyle

Leaping
Revelations and Epiphanies
$14.95 • Paperback • 3904-5

In *Leaping*, a spirited, tumbling, and passionate collection of essays, Brian Doyle employs wit and cheerful verve to explore a myriad of Catholic topics, from the intricate genius and theater of the Mass, to Jesus' pointy elbows, to the relentless, joyous curiosity of children—and so much more.

In his playful and distinctly clever voice, Doyle ponders the sweet madness of forgiveness, other names we might confer on Jesus, and the *real* point of praying when it feels empty and shallow at the time. From the serious to the hilarious, Doyle masterfully weaves stories that make you grin, weep, remember, reflect, and perhaps plunge anew, refreshed, into your own leaps of faith.

TO ORDER: Call 800.621.1008, visit loyolapress.com/store or visit your local bookseller.